WORDS OUT
OF SILENCE

Quietness and conflict, life and death, place and memory, politics and pity, friendship and peace. In *Words Out of Silence,* Jill Segger weaves a tapestry of poetry and prose that takes us on journeys of personal transformation set against (and responsive to) the backdrop of turmoil in the world around us. The common ground of the words in this book is silence, and specifically the silence of the Quaker Meeting. This is the source of its deep humanity: something that will appeal both to those who see themselves as 'religious' and those who do not.

Jill Segger is a writer and an active member of the Religious Society of Friends (Quakers). She has a particular interest in how spirituality influences our social and political choices. Jill began contributing to the work of Ekklesia in March 2009, and became an associate director in 2010. She is also a composer.

This book will speak not just to people who consider themselves 'religious', but to many who do not; to Quakers and to those of different traditions – Christian and otherwise – who are searching for connectedness and humility in a world of increasing division and hubris.

Simon Barrow, Director of Ekklesia

It is in her poems' interplay with her prose that Jill Segger shows the power of words to speak truth. Her prose is personal, political and passionate.

Rachel Mann, writing in the Foreword

To the memory of my parents who taught me to love both words and silence

WORDS OUT OF SILENCE

Jill Segger

Ekklesia

First published in May 2019

Ekklesia
235 Shaftesbury Avenue
London
WC2H 8EP
www.ekklesia.co.uk

Production and design: Bob Carling (www.carling.org.uk)
Managing Editor: Simon Barrow

ISBN: 978-0-9932942-8-0

The cover: the coloured glass on the front was photographed at the Newbury meeting of the Mid Thames area Quakers (https://midthamesquakers.org.uk), to whom we give grateful acknowledgement and thanks.

A Catalogue record for this book is available from the British Library.

This is the first title in a new Ekklesia imprint called Siglum (a sign or symbol that can represent a word or name). The imprint focuses on the illuminative and transformative possibilities of the arts, music and culture in both religious and secular contexts. Its logo is a dove, the universal sign of peace.

Contents

Publisher's Preface

It is a particular pleasure to publish this modest but significant volume of poetry and prose by Jill Segger – whose friendship, wisdom and professional expertise many of us in Ekklesia have been privileged to share during the best part of a decade.

As Jill says in her own introduction to thoughts generated over a number of years, and offered both as verse and as commentary: "The common ground of the words in this book is silence, and specifically the silence of the Quaker Meeting for Worship." The activities of prayer and worship are normative disciplines for many people from different backgrounds and faiths. They are ways of rooting ourselves in a larger story, a wider set of relationships and, yes, a greater Silence. Yet for many in today's over-busy world, they seem strange and out of place. Perhaps, however, it is the habits of an unequal, unjust and inhospitable 'consumer society' which are the real cause of our sense of dis-ease, while the strange gifts of silence and disarmed words can be – as they are here – sources of healing and repair.

Reading through this inspiring collection one is reminded, again and again, that our shared humanity is both immensely valuable and incredibly fragile. So *Words Out of Silence* continually takes us back to those reservoirs of hope, peace, joy and justice which are the work of true prayer and authentic spirituality. This book will speak not just to people who consider themselves 'religious', but to many who do not; to Quakers and to those of different traditions – Christian and otherwise – who are searching for connectedness and humility in a world of increasing division and hubris.

Ekklesia is delighted to have the opportunity to offer in collected form, and to a wider audience, some of Jill Segger's writings which have moved and inspired people since 2009, as well as poems that evoke vital truths in a different way. You will find this a profoundly political but non-partisan book. Above all it is committed to that openness to silence which is also the hallmark of artistic sensibility. That is something we are committed to exploring in greater depth as part of the 'thought space' which Ekklesia seeks to offer, and for which this collection is an entirely appropriate gateway.

Simon Barrow
Director, Ekklesia

Foreword

A little distance into *Words Out of Silence,* Jill Segger suggests that "Quakers are not generally theologians, systematic or otherwise. We tend more towards theopoetics – those qualities of allegory which, as with poetry, may take on different and new meanings throughout life as the changing reader experiences the fluid text." It is one of those statements that reveals not only Jill's gift for language and poetic effect, but (as I would put it) her skills as a theologian. It is out of these curious and supple ironies that this fascinating, moving and timely book emerges.

In the popular mind, Quakers have a reputation as people gifted around silence. There are good reasons for this. Worshipping in the manner of the Society of Friends entails a quietening of one's frenetic mind and restless body in order to connect with the power of silence to call forth words that matter. Quakers know that to speak, to break the silence, is always risky. It may lead to foolishness, cheap anger and frivolity.

Jill Segger's meditations and poems are the very opposite of foolish and frivolous. At their heart is a preparedness to wait for the right moment to speak; what one finds when Segger speaks is a quiet passion, a sober, but never pious seriousness. *Words Out of Silence* draws words from across many years of experience and reflection and its themes indicate the author's abiding concerns: friendship and justice, gift and grace, peace and mercy. In her meditations on ageing and death, one finds deep wisdom and a commitment to living simply and generously. In our disposable, self and selfie-obsessed age, her quality of attention is startling.

It is tempting to claim that those who are attentive to quietness and silence are committed to quietism. For those unaware of Jill Segger's (and indeed wider Quaker) thought, *Words Out of Silence* will supply a shock. She reminds us that "In 1987, Quakers in Britain issued a declaration ahead of the General Election which returned Margaret Thatcher to her third term in government. It contained these words: 'We commit ourselves to learning again the spiritual value of each other. We find ourselves utterly at odds with the priorities in our society which deny the full human potential of millions of people in this country. That denial diminishes us all. There must be no 'them' and 'us'.'" One of the most potent seams running through *Words Out of Silence* is therefore a fierce determination to keep face-to-face, body-to-body, skin-to-skin, with those who are regarded as of secondary value in the UK and beyond.

Part of the power of Jill Segger's writing lies in its careful balance between the demands of poetry and prose. Her poetry is discrete and controlled. The Quaker poets R.V. Bailey and Stevie Krayer recently said (in a volume devoted to Quaker poets), "poetry is about trying to tell the truth". Jill works hard to keep to that territory, but it is in her poems' interplay with her prose that she shows the power of words to speak truth. Her prose is personal, political and passionate. As she says, "It has been well said that peace is not the absence of noise, trouble or hard work – rather it is to be in the midst of those things and still be calm in your heart." It is a truth more of us would do well to learn.

Rachel Mann
May 2019

Author's Preface

From deep within a hack, a poet may eventually scrabble towards the light. This does not imply that the prose which pays the bills is an inferior form to poetry, but that it speaks to a writer's exploration of difference and similarity which, if internalised and permitted to grow, has the potential to enrich both forms of expression.

The ordering of words is a discipline of mind and ear. In that sense, poetry differs from comment journalism principally in the intensity of its distillation and, in what may seem to contradict that quality, the unloosing which gives the reader leave to engage with what is offered in allusion and ambiguity. That space, becoming a tool which will eventually sit securely in the writer's hand, may serve to enlarge the language of comment.

Of course, comment belongs to a particular time and, except on those rare occasions when it may encompass something beyond that frame, cannot hope for a long shelf-life. Poetry also takes a moment in time but seeks its wider application in the fixing of a personal experience. This is where the poet must exercise humility and faith, neither assuming that the particular may be taken as universal, nor losing hope in the possibility that it may nonetheless transcend individual difference by slowing the beat of our lives a little and unlatching a door into something we had forgotten to remember.

The common ground of the words in this book is silence, and specifically the silence of the Quaker Meeting for Worship. It is in this collective and attentive waiting on the Spirit that what had hitherto not been fully known may begin to stir in a space apart from that of the conscious and discursive self.

What germinates in this manner will later present itself to that faculty of my mind which must engage to develop, execute and deliver the written product. These events are not necessarily sequential but they are always coherent and I have learned that I must trust the interconnection of faith and practice which they represent. This is the heart of Quakerism.

I am daughter and grand-daughter of woodworkers and seamstresses; great-grand-daughter of a landscape gardener. Making is in my genes. The impulse to offer something which was not there before is strong. As is the hope that of what is made, a little may perhaps outlive my telomeres. Whether this book may prove such an artefact, only time will show.

Acknowledgements

I am grateful to my Ekklesia colleagues and friends: Simon Barrow, who received the idea of this book with enthusiasm and has been supportive throughout, and Bernadette Meaden who provided invaluable clarity where I was fogged.

My thanks are also due to Ekklesia, which has, for almost 10 years, given me the freedom to write as the Spirit leads me, and to Bury St Edmunds Quaker Meeting which has made possible most of the generative silence.

Jill Segger
May 2019

In Quiet Places

Approaching Silence

Do not press
at the doorway into silence.
That you are here means it has opened.
Stand, maybe hang back
upon the step,
stoop a little to attentiveness.

This is how you make
the intake into
ground.

Turbulent times and the sound of a thin silence
October 2, 2017

The theme of National Quaker week 2017 is 'In turbulent times...be a Quaker'. The Society of Friends has also issued an 'invitation to stillness'.

Turbulence and stillness: these apparently opposed conditions present an ongoing challenge. Turbulence is all around us; stillness and its essential component of silence are less easy to find but they are vital for our individual and collective health and for our capacity to respond to turbulence without increasing it.

Silence has many faces and it is worth considering its negative aspects as well as its life-giving qualities. There is the silence of fear, of collusion and concealment. We will all have experienced the silence of embarrassment. Most of us will also know the temptation to 'keep quiet' because not doing so would oblige us to commitment we may not be willing to undertake. These are the stamps of a silence which adds to personal and collective turbulence.

Then there are the silences of our shared history which must never be forgotten and for which there can be no words: the first silence of 1918, the silence of Auschwitz.

There are questions too. Is silence simply the absence of sound? Does it generate meaning or simply make meaning possible? Are we prepared for its subversive possibilities, for its capacity to mess with our expectations and prejudices?

Silence is at the heart of Quaker spiritual experience. The 'gathered silence' for which we hope in our worship can be challenging. Sometimes mundane qualities like feeling fidgety or preoccupied can impede us. On other occasions, we may resist entering into the silence because we are apprehensive as to what we may find there. We are part of a culture which often uses noise as concealment, a distraction from the unpalatable or disturbing. The 'always on' television, the ubiquitous personal music player, the musical wallpaper of shops, eating places and waiting rooms – these generally unquestioned practices are ultimately isolating and disabling. We cease to hear quietness as a precursor to true silence and are deprived of the experience and therefore the recognition that silence and stillness are skills which we need to practise.

The 'still, small voice' experience of Elijah (1 Kings, 19. 12-13) is often quoted as an instance of the silence of the Divine confounding our expectations. But that familiar version may mislead us. The original

3

Hebrew is better translated as 'the sound of a thin silence'. There are two aspects here which speak to my condition. Silence perceived as possessing a quality of sound offers a paradox which invites me to creative co-operation. (Thank you Simon and Garfunkel). And the concept of thinness – not shallowness – is akin to the 'thin places' of Celtic spirituality: locations where the quotidian borders between the material and spiritual realms are suddenly made flimsy. It is in such places and through such experiences that we may find the rumour of God taking form, despite our preoccupation with scepticism and disbelief.

The turbulence around us is very real. Anti-democratic violence has erupted in Spain. The criminally irresponsible war of insults between Donald Trump and Kim Jong-un inches the world closer to nuclear conflict. The fall-out of the Brexit referendum with its scarifying abuse on both sides is dividing families, communities and political parties. The ineptitude and mendacity of many whom we elect to represent and govern us generates cynical alienation. Many of our fellow citizens are forced to live in deprivation and fear and this is a deep shame upon us all. We are disturbed, fearful, often angry. We are damaging ourselves badly by total immersion in a world of constant information divorced from wisdom. We are not helpless but we have to find a remedy for the fear that we are.

On 1 September 1939, as German troops invaded Poland, WH Auden wrote:

> The lights must never go out,
> The music must always play,
> All the conventions conspire
> To make this fort assume
> The furniture of home,
> Lest we should see where we are,
> Lost in a haunted wood;
> Children afraid of the night
> Who have never been happy or good.

If we can sometimes dare to turn off the music, to embrace darkness, to enter on the unfamiliar place, in short, to risk the unfamiliar and counter-cultural, silence and stillness may enable a growing understanding of possibility. This is the territory where respite from bickering and insult and release from the futility of ego-driven conflict can be found. It is not an escape, but it is a portal to the transformative.

A time to speak and a time to be silent
June 20, 2016

Sometimes only silence will serve. On the Friday evening following the murder of Jo Cox on the street outside her constituency surgery, I was among a group of Quakers who gathered to hold the MP, her family and our country in the Light.

There was no discussion, no planning of future action. There was only wordless waiting on the Spirit, the holding of a space where the edge could be taken off anger, hostility and fear; where gaps could be bridged and remaking become a possibility. In this space, we could share our shock and sorrow without recourse to words which might, even inadvertently, have hardened into resentment and thus into impediments to reconciliation.

The EU referendum campaign was suspended until the following Sunday and my initial response was to wish that it would not resume, leaving the remaining days before the poll to reflection and exploration of facts without further noise and vitriol.

However, despite the ugliness of the resumption and the horrifying attempts of Nigel Farage to justify the 'breaking point' immigration poster by accusing his opponents of 'using' Jo Cox's death, I have changed my mind. Debate is the lifeblood of democracy and to close it down would to have been to acquiesce in the power of violence to silence freedom. There is a time to speak and a time to be silent.

But silence is essential to finding a way towards the speech which will open a way forward. The killing of Jo Cox was not only an attack upon a young mother which has left a family broken, but also on the very nature of representative democracy. It is very easy to be drawn into the frenzy of outrage and shouting which has followed this terrible event – to be seduced by clickbait attempts to recruit us to a particular stance and to forget that if division on the current level continues, there can be no good outcome.

The courts will deal with the charge on which Thomas Mair is arraigned. We can at least keep silent about that on social media and temper our language away from venom and revenge in private conversation. We can choose to dial down on the angry rhetoric on both sides of the debate and seek to find a more civil and productive discourse in these last days before the poll.

Above all, we must keep in mind that after 23 June, we have to live together. There will be bridges to be built and if the result is – as seems likely – very close, how we use silence over the coming three days may be the difference between the kind of society Jo Cox worked so hard to build and a descent into further conflict. "She saw no one as a permanent enemy", said her fellow MP Stephen Doughty. Let us do no less.

Reflections at a time of inauguration
January 23, 2017

The inauguration of an American president is a unique mix of razzmatazz and nobility. It is the nobility which must not be lost sight of and which may yet give us hope.

When the former colony set out its founding principles and rules of governance almost two and a half centuries ago, it was striving to give form to something which had never been tried before – the making of an independent democracy that had cast off the structures of empire and was straining upwards in hope and with courage

Despite its failures over that time, despite its excursions into blind alleys of war and injustice and despite the human weaknesses – even criminality in some instances – of the men who have held the office of president in this new form of society, it yet retains at least the potential of being "a shining city on a hill". I believe this to be why the inauguration of Donald Trump has horrified and cast so many around the world into deep anxiety.

But analysis of the 45th President's character and of his inauguration speech is for another comment piece. On Friday 20 January 2017, a small group from the Quaker Meeting of which I am a member came together in a Friend's home to hold silence during the ceremony in Washington DC.

As we entered into the silence, the late afternoon light died out of the sky, draining it through azure to copper, then to almost black until the faint starlight of a wintry night settled over the Suffolk landscape. It was odd to think that daylight from the same sun which had gone out of our sight still stood over the ceremonial district of the USA's capital city. Odder still, though of great comfort, to know that people from across the United Kingdom and the USA had tweeted me to say they were joining us in their spirits. There was – is – a real need to be silent a while and to reflect beyond the anger and fear that fills newspaper columns, air waves and social media.

We needed to be silent for a space, for Donald Trump, for the divided people of the United States and for ourselves. Despair and rage are powerfully contagious but they have a limited utility. It is beyond doubt that we need to prepare ourselves for right resistance and to be ready for conflict, its resolution and healing.

I can offer no route plan for this journey. We are still in the early stages of shock. But I do know that unless we go within, we will not well go outward. And in our silent gathering, I remembered the challenge George Fox offered in a Cumbrian parish church in 1652 when he rose in his seat to cry out to the congregation: "What canst thou say?"

Not what do we say, what will we say, but what *can* we say? It is for everyone of us to find and recognise the unique capacity to which that calls us. And then to combine in an alternative narrative. We will wear a coat of many colours but if we will listen well, it could be a seamless robe.

Quaker Meeting at Haughley Barn

Music will spring from silence, take its way and in
falling to the necessary cadence, breathe.
Shaped by notself, just as mass and space have no meaning
apart, quietness emerges from the spring afternoon.
Precursor of silence only, the stillness is imperfect.
Pheasants clatter to flight; a small air moves on
brick and leaf; we shift and settle, quelling inattention.
Ancient timber frames the space of our waiting and
we too, are parentheses.

Attentive waiting, beauty and hope: trying what Advent will do
December 8, 2017

Lying awake, waiting for first light, longing for some deliverance from fear, pain, despair, helplessness, lassitude. These are experiences that few will escape at some time in their lives. They are characteristic of much that is human. They are also the notes of this overlooked season of Advent.

I belong to a faith group which does not heed a liturgical calendar. We worship as the spirit leads us. Nonetheless, I have long felt Advent to be a rather Quakerly season. It has always been our way to watch, to listen, and to wait in attentive hope. This is the spring of our action, both personal and corporate.

The Advent liturgies of mainstream Christianity and their cultural off-shoots speak to my experience and condition. Darkling sentinels watch and long for the light. The watchman wonders when the night will pass. The prophets call from the desert. The people dwell in darkness but cling to a barely believable hope that a Dayspring will dawn on their desolate condition.

Quakers are not generally theologians, systematic or otherwise. We tend more towards theopoetics – those qualities of allegory which, as with poetry, may take on different and new meanings throughout life as the changing reader experiences the fluid text.

This concept of 'text' is wide. The spirit, being that of a creator, may address us in poetry, scripture, music, visual art, or in those moments of extasis, which, even as we return to our everyday standing place, we may simultaneously welcome and doubt.

This theologically ungrammatical approach is not mainstream in 'organised' religion. But in its looking to humankind's natural harmony with that which is beyond its own doctrinal prescriptions, it is neither anti-intellectual nor dangerously subjective. Drawing on the most enduring representations of the beauty which is both ancient and new, it is rooted in millennia of attention to the Divine spirit, however we may choose to name that concept.

Advent, with its multi-layered message, has been largely replaced by 'the run up to Christmas' in our present culture. The attentive waiting, the promise of a time yet to come, on which Isaiah called out in prophetic hope: "Drop down, ye heavens, from above, and let the skies pour down righteousness: let the earth open, and let them bring forth salvation, and let righteousness spring up together", is more complex and demanding than carols playing on a loop, tinsel and Yuletide sentimentality. Waiting and listening are not attributes highly valued by the advertisers and hucksters who want to sell us a Nativity which can at best, be a temporary displacement activity.

So, bruised and crushed by injustice, suffering, conflict, wars and tempted to despair though yearning to hope, let us try what the Advent spirit will do. Whatever is beautiful, less familiar, ancient but eternal, within our reach, if not always our grasp – let's try to make that our path for the next 16 days.

Knowing one another in the things that are eternal
December 20, 2010

Quakers don't really 'do' Christmas. Partly in order to offer a sign of contradiction to the consumerism and commercialism of the season which is in conflict with our Testimony to simplicity; partly because we believe that all of life and all its days and times are sacramental; partly because there is such a wide range of views in the Society of Friends as to the nature of the man Jesus.

But we are also drawn to acknowledging and, in some form joining with, the communal experiences which mark these days, and to drawing from the wells of wisdom and reflection which the tradition has to offer. So it was that on the last Sunday before Christmas, the Meeting of which I am a member, worshipped for half an hour in the usual format of silent attentiveness to the leadings of the divine spirit and then – varying the customary practice of our weekly gathering – offered 'gifts to the tree'. This consists of writing a short reflection, prayer, quotation or hope for the coming year on a tag which Friends then hang on the Christmas tree whilst offering a brief exposition of their choice.

We heard of experiences of suffering transformed by hope; of reflection upon individual Friends' experiences; of joy at new life, gratitude for light in times of literal and metaphoric darkness and of unlooked for transformation in unpromising circumstances. Our oldest Friend, in a voice ringing with certainty and a strength which belied her 95 years, reminded us of the beautiful phrase from John's gospel about the "dayspring from on high" whilst our newest member challenged the government to formulate policy with justice and compassion. Another Friend, his speech quavering a little with emotion, spoke of his desire that as a businessman he might play an active part in striving for integrity in financial dealings.

In the coming days, as I struggle with deadlines and try not to succumb to irritation and despondency in the search for parking places and brussel sprouts, I realise how blessed I am to spend time amongst people who, in George Fox's words, strive always to "know one another in the things that are eternal".

Music Room

Late winter light scrolls brightwork on the silent piano;
slants, dust-dancing over a page of Bach.

Sound seeds, rich as grapes, wait upon hands' husbandry,
but the air does not fruit.

Germinating doubt, the pianist is in the garden.

Digging.

The Drones Quilt: stitching for Noor
April 29, 2013

Last Saturday, demonstrators gathered for a protest march at RAF Waddington in Lincolnshire from where drone attacks on Afghanistan are now controlled. On 7 May, the Drones Quilt – a project initiated by the Fellowship of Reconciliation – will be handed in at Downing Street. Between these two events, I heard a moving ministry from a Friend who had participated in making a square for the quilt.

The concept put forward by the Fellowship of Reconciliation – supported by peace groups across the country – is simple. Each square is stitched with the name of a human being killed by a drone attack. Its purpose is to restore humanity to those appearing on lists as killed or maimed and to remind people, especially those in power, that "for every single victim of a drone there was a real person with loves, desires and a life."

Mag, like me, is no needlewoman. She told Meeting for Worship that she chose eight-year-old Noor Sayed for her square because the name was short and would not make too many demands on her limited skills. Nonetheless, it took longer that she had expected and as she pricked her fingers, dropped pins and tangled the thread, she found herself reflecting more and more on the child whose name she was picking out in blue wool and whose death in Pakistan in 2009 was categorised as 'collateral damage'.

She wondered about Noor's appearance – was her hair straight or curly? Her nature – was she quiet and serious or mischievous and lively? What did her parents do for a living? What was their house like? And what was she doing in the moments before a drone-launched missile took her so brutally out of a life scarcely begun?

Mag googled for the meaning of the name 'Noor' and found it meant 'light'. Her own daughter's name has the same meaning. As she struggled through her stitching, she felt a growing sense of closeness to the child from so far away. I think none of us who heard Mag's witness will forget it. In a Quaker Meeting House in East Anglia, little Noor had become Everychild.

If only politicians, pilots and generals could be encouraged to sit quietly and struggle with something they find difficult to execute. It might just give them the space to reflect that in armed conflict, all whom we kill are our own.

Wondering again over the Passion
April 22, 2011

On the Tuesday of Holy Week, I was privileged to undergo an extraordinary cultural experience. That it was also deeply moving and provoked me into fresh reflection on the enduring meaning of the wretched betrayal and execution of a Palestinian Rabbi, was due to the melding of so many traditions, times and unique skills in one unforgettable performance.

The occasion was a performance of Bach's St John Passion in Kings College, Cambridge. That is to say, a setting by an 18th century German composer of a translation into his own tongue of a Greek account of the trial and execution of an Iron Age Mediterranean religious radical, performed in a 15th century English church.

Bach wrote this work for the Good Friday liturgy at the Lutheran Nikolaikirche in Leipzig. Ears grown used to more overt drama and lesser constraints, must be willing to listen outside modern expectations for insight into suffering portrayed within the conventions of a very different age.

King's College choir, the masterly Academy of Ancient Music and all the soloists performed with immense skill and power. It seems invidious to pick out individuals. But the singing of David Wilson-Johnson as Jesus, and Andrew Kennedy in the technically demanding role of the Evangelist – the engine of the narrative movement – had that rare quality, far beyond accomplishment, which comes from utter conviction.

When Wilson-Johnson left his last phrase "Es ist vollbracht!" (it is finished) hanging so quietly in the air of the Chapel, the silence which followed was charged with a shared emotion that bound the capacity audience with almost unbearable intensity. The singer's head fell to one side and his body seemed to crumple as though the slackness of death had come upon him also. Whatever one's beliefs about the person of Jesus and the meaning of his death, this was a moment when the universality of the Passion narrative stood plain for all to see.

That this narrative has endured and spread throughout the world, inspiring music, art, drama, and architecture in so many different cultures while still retaining its essential shape, is unique. Because we in the 'Christian' west have been familiar with it for so long, it may become attenuated. That is presumably why the liturgical dramas of the 'Great Week' seek to re-enact and revivify the 'old, old story' in every generation, in every culture.

The humanity of Jesus and his death open a gateway into faith for me. Though adhering to the Quaker belief that "we take our inspiration from Jesus but refrain from making dogmatic statements about him", I still hold him to be a uniquely inspired and God-filled individual. What I heard and witnessed (in what some of my co-religionists would call a 'steeple-house') two days ago, in reinforcing my sense of wonder at the deep levels of skill, co-operation and negation of self which make possible the rebirth and re-presentation of what is timeless, taught me something new.

Neither the Palestinian working men who followed Jesus nor the military-political power machine which killed him, would have been unable to make any point of contact with the height of Baroque musical genius which sang their story in Cambridge this week. The finely made reproductions of 18th century flutes, viola da gamba and oboe di amore would have been meaningless objects to them. The great vaulted ceiling of Henry VI's chapel and its crocketted, pinnacled exterior would probably not have been recognisable as a place of worship.

We have the advantage. We have taken their experience and passed it through centuries of creativity and re-interpretation. This cultural, artistic and creative hybrid has huge vitality. But if is not to trap us in an aesthetic dead end, we must use its energy to take us back to the source so we may look again and again with eyes cleared by wonder.

Mercy, Pity, Peace and Love

Brief Encounter

On the station concourse I saw a young man broken.
He had leaned towards her, hunched and pliant in pleading,
his hands like frightened birds that dared not alight.
And when she turned from him with swinging step,
anguish angled his body as though his breath had been taken.

I longed to hold him and shield his weeping;
to tell him that joy was not gone for ever and there would be
other loves –
but knew it for a half truth.
First rejection re-calibrates the innocent heart;
messengers of loss slip within the gates
and we are unparadised.

Anders Behring Breivik and Dr Ali
July 24, 2011

On the day that Anders Behring Breivik, driven by hatred of Islam and of his country's political establishment, unleashed death and terror on an unimaginable scale in Oslo and Utoya, I lay on a treatment table in the Accident and Emergency department of my local hospital. The doctor attending to my pain and shock was a gentle young Muslim called Ali.

I had tripped and fallen in the street, dislocating my elbow and generally battering my face. Ali, softly spoken and with the kindest eyes an anxious patient could wish to see, placed a canula into my hand and said "are you OK, Jill?". I confessed to being a little frightened. Ali took my uninjured hand, "We will look after you" he whispered.

As morphine was administered, I talked with Ali. He was from Sudan, had studied medicine in Hungary and was now working in A&E in this small Suffolk town. "It is nice town" he said. "All people are friendly".

The anaesthetist warned that the sedative they would use while resetting my elbow gave rise to rather hallucinatory effects on regaining consciousness, "so try to find some pleasant thoughts as you go under", he advised. Turning to Ali, I asked him to tell me about his children. His pleasure was evident and I learned that his wife and children, would soon be joining him in England after a separation of seven months.

"They are good children" he told me, "Two little girls and a boy. They are kind and very sensitive". That did not surprise me. He told me that the boy was named Osama, "But not like the bad one". Ali's best friend, also called Osama, had died in a drowning accident, "so I call my boy for love of his memory".

He continued to talk to me as I slid into unconsciousness and the last thing I remember registering were his wise words about allowing children to save as much face as was compatible with necessary obedience.

Later, Ali came to see me in recovery and we talked a little more about faith and love. He had not heard of Quakers, so for simplicity's sake, I told him that we worship in silence and are dedicated to peace. "Ah, good. Peace is good" he said, smiling and nodding his head. I thanked him for his care and wished him blessing, for himself and his family. He touched my face and caressed my shoulder in a manner which would not have been possible for a European man to do without seeming over familiar. It was his blessing.

I believe that what was shown to me by Ali went beyond the care a doctor gives to an injured patient. We had made contact on a very human level and it was the tacit acknowledgement of the God whom we call by different names and worship in different ways which enhanced that experience.

For me, Ali was the true face of Islam. It is easier to understand something of which we may have limited or partial knowledge when we find it incarnated in an individual of transparent goodness. It is Anders Brehing Breivik's tragedy that he has either never had that encounter or permitted himself to believe in the possibility of its existence.

Hospital Visit

There are few words between them.
– You shouldn't have come –
He is fretful at the overthrow of sixty years shared strength;
she endures, the flecked, knuckly hands make no gesture.

There will be an unlocking of tenderness in the last few minutes.
But not yet.
She has learned patience.

999 Convention for the NHS: common frailty, shared humanity
December 13, 2014

There are few of us who either enter or leave this world without its presence. In between, the NHS is there for broken bones, depression, ingrowing toenails, heart attacks, cancer and all the diverse pain, fear and suffering of our lives' journeys.

It does not always get everything right. But for a huge amount of the time, it mends, saves, soothes and supports our frailties. And it does all this without sending us an invoice. Still free at the point of delivery, as established by the social visionaries of the 1945 Labour government, but increasingly under threat from a neo-liberal administration, the NHS is a deeply humane and civilised institution.

A couple of days ago, I took a friend to the outpatient department of a large hospital for a radiotherapy appointment. This treatment generally comes after surgery and in many cases, after chemotherapy. The people gathered in rows of pale blue chairs, quiet and private behind carefully composed faces, were all in the process of dealing with one of the most devastating diagnoses any of us can receive. Many had travelled considerable distances and would do so daily for at least 15 sessions. There were no complaints and no signs of impatience, though most of the five treatment units were running about 40 minutes late.

There was something profoundly touching to me about being present among these people who had suffered considerably and were entrusting themselves to the technology, skills and compassion of our publicly funded health service. Their chances of life and their futures were focused on this place and the care it provides. The snatches of conversation I heard, and my friend's discourse, were all centred on gratitude and relief: "they've looked after me so well", "we can't be thankful enough...", "they're all so kind."

But this unique organisation is already being fragmented and made subject to competition and market forces by a government which truly knows the cost of everything and the value of nothing. It is not the purpose of this present piece to explore the idiocy and cruelty of hostility to our remarkable system of state funded health care, but it does seem a good moment to draw attention to the 999 Call for Change campaign.

This invites all NHS campaigners, activists, trade unions and concerned citizens to join together in a National Convention to Save the NHS in England and Wales.

The idea for the 999 Convention for the NHS grew out of the 999 People's March for the NHS from Jarrow to London which took place during August and September. On its journey through 23 towns and cities, the march united trade unionists, councillors, politicians, pensioners groups, health campaigners and local communities in defence of the NHS.

Realising that such diverse layers of support could be weakened by fragmentation, the organisers looked for a means of providing a united voice and of coordinating days of action in the run-up to the General Election, putting the NHS at the centre of the election campaign and preparing the ground for campaigning beyond it.

They say: "We want the mass protests in defence of hospitals in Lewisham and Stafford, united with the determination of the 999 Marchers, combined with the energy and direct action of UK Uncut and tax avoidance campaigners, occupying banks and blocking bridges to protect the NHS. The convention will be a chance to discuss the way forward, agree days of action before the General Election and organise a national campaigning body to continue to defend the NHS whichever party wins the general election."

They emphasise that the convention is open to all who want to defend the founding principles of the NHS. Discussions have taken place with key figures from other organisations including Keep our NHS Public (KONP), National Health Action Party, and local NHS campaign groups who have already indicated support.

We all use the NHS. We all need it. A moment's inattention on a motorway, a few rogue cells in the viscera and our lives will depend on its dedication and skill. As the General Election approaches, it is well to remember Aneurin Bevan's words: "It will last as long as there are folk left with the faith to fight for it."

Now is the time to show faith in the organisation that is perhaps the ultimate witness to our common frailty and to the best of our shared humanity.

Simplicity and freedom
April 5, 2011

"'Tis the gift to be simple, 'tis the gift to be free". The Shaker hymn has always been dear to me; not least because its open-spaced and perfectly poised melody makes such a perfect fit with the spirit of the plain, graceful words.

The concept of freedom being contingent upon simplicity runs counter to the received wisdom of our culture which, acting as the servant of consumer capitalism, would have us believe that it is by acquisition that we attain freedom; that our possessions (and by extension, our purchasing power) are the only indicators of our personal value and therefore of an individualism which has come to be considered as inseparable from freedom.

Bur freedom is far too precious to leave this conflation unquestioned and simplicity far too multi-faceted to be dismissed as a hair-shirt eccentricity of dissenters with leanings towards 17th century radicalism.

To be in thrall to materialism is an obvious defect and one which most people of good faith try to avoid to some degree. For myself, the pre-purchase test "do I need this or do I just want it?" works fairly well in most purely acquisitive situations. But the avoidance of 'cumber' is only part of the struggle to live a simple life.

Perhaps more important is the constant need to re-shape desires and to discern their motivation. 'Keeping up with the Joneses' is both more readily identified and more obviously risible than is the defect of falling victim to 'group-think' – a state of mind to which we are all vulnerable. Being 'in' with one's personal, social and professional peers is important to most of us and the capacity to know when to step away and seek clarity (the seedbed of principled dissent) is of the greatest importance. The frame of mind and heart which makes this possible seems to me to depend on that particular simplicity which Jesus called "purity of heart".

That blessed condition is not easy to define but it is unmistakeable when encountered. It sees past self-interest, is immune to manipulation, clear-sighted about weakness and always forbearing – forgiving of others and of self. It is never deluded but neither does it become cynical. If we have known individuals in our lives who display these qualities, then we share in the benison.

But maybe it is necessary to start with questioning our own material temptations in order to clear the doors of perception. It is when I have truly understood that I don't live by bread alone (or by high-tech gizmos and good wine) that I may just get near enough to what Friends call 'clearness' to understand my real needs, the needs of my neighbours and the part I must play in answering those needs.

The Shaker hymn 'Simple Gifts' concludes that it is by "turning, turning, that we come out right". So during what is left of Lent, I am resolved to rotate in search of true freedom.

25 December 2016

We give ourselves so much trouble
with the G word.
Angry at long-ago misleading, still half feart at an
Ancient of Days marking our book, we
waste ourselves.

Leave be. Still be.
There is love downdeep, star-moving spark
banked heavy but ready to blaze into fulfilment
if we will mend our hearths.

Emmanuel.

Reflections from a Quaker household on the time called Christmas
December 24, 2015

As early as I can remember, and certainly before I had words for the concept, I have known that there is a string in the human psyche which is placed to vibrate in sympathy with a frequency generated beyond our material and circadian existence.

This was not the kind of knowledge gained from organised instruction. It was just there. An awareness, at times all but obscured, but at others as plain as my own hands and feet, of the Divine 'other'. In childhood, it would mostly come unlooked for in moments of solitude, and frequently in unlikely surroundings – the flight of green, mossy steps joining our back yard to that of the bakery next door was a place of encounter, as was the tiny shed on my grandfather's allotment with its fragrance of earth, wood and vegetables.

These days, I find it best in the gathered quiet of a Meeting for Worship and in the reverent attention due to poetry, great music or the beauty of the natural world. It comes in stillness and eludes me when I am surrounded by noise and activity. Not that there is anything intrinsically wrong with these conditions and indeed, I welcome the necessary stimulation and companionship they offer. I am neither a mystic nor an anchoress.

But sometimes, the string hums gently amid daily busyness and the tentative harmonics call me to clear the doors of perception. This season called Christmas is such a time.

Quakers tend to keep a more low-key Christmas than is the social norm. We have no liturgies nor do we believe that any time or season is more 'holy' than another. If we heed the Nativity, it is in a way which has as little as possible to do with the trappings which the commercial and advertising world would have us believe are essential.

So for this household, there has been no present buying, no storing in of rich food, no dressing of a tree nor singing of carols. This is not joyless puritanism – we don't condemn, we just choose otherwise. And in so choosing, I find myself alert to those quiet harmonic overtones which can so easily go unheard beneath the sound of a less true string echoing to what advertising culture encourages us to call 'the magic of Christmas'.

That echo may be distorted but nonetheless, it owes its existence to the 'otherness' of a unique night and its enduring myth. And here, I insist upon the real meaning of that word: not a synonym for falsehood, but a story told about truth.

The story of the Nativity sounds deep to truth. For that reason, masterpieces of visual art, literature and music have been closely entwined with it for centuries. Despite appropriation in the cause of 'feel-good' purchasing, these withstand changing times because they are close to that authentically taut string which waits for the touch that will set it in motion.

So on this night when the circle of the eternal – in a way I experience but for which I have no explanation – comes very close to the orbit of the temporal, the small but insistent hum in my spirit is amplified by these words from the Wisdom of Solomon: "All things were lying in peace and silence, and night in her swift course was half spent, when thine almighty Word leapt from thy royal throne in heaven."

Let us make room at the inn of our own hearts. A world where violence is the stock response to conflict needs it; a political and economic system which so often values self-seeking above compassion and truth needs it; every single one of us, whatever our rank, condition or allegiance, needs it. We might not 'believe' after the manner of creeds and catechisms, but if we listen for that deep note, rather than seeking to feel 'Christmassy', then perhaps, like the shepherds and kings of UA Fanthorpe's beautiful poem BC:AD, we may find we have walked "haphazard by starlight into the kingdom of heaven."

Hope, myth and a small god
December 23, 2016

Early this month, I heard one woman say to another at a supermarket checkout "It doesn't feel Christmassy yet". I resisted the temptation to say that was because it was barely Advent, but I have been wondering since what 'Christmassy' might mean in 2016.

As the least attractive manifestations of this season intensify in sparkles, twinkles, John Lewis ads and Away in a Manger playing on a supermarket loop, it seems that a soft-focus sentimentality has become the 'Christmassy' defence against the grim realities of a world which appears to be spinning ever faster into division, conflict, cruelty and untruth.

Christmas has shown itself adaptable over the centuries, from the fourth century adoption of a pagan festival to underpin the narrative of Nativity, through the Victorian modulations of Prince Albert and Charles Dickens, to our present day festival of stressed-out consumerism and yearning sentimentality.

In this tradition, we need to discover – or perhaps rediscover – an understanding for our own time. In losing the concept of myth, we have stranded ourselves between two stools, neither of which can fully bear the weight of our weary limbs. Language evolves and words

28

shift their meaning but as 'myth' becomes synonymous with 'lie', both fundamentalists and cynics are trapped in mutual hostilities and the hungry flock looks up, unfed.

A myth could not be further from a lie. It is a story told about truth. It will have drawn on some elements of historic fact but clothes these in the imaginative and symbolic to give them a poetic trajectory into our hearts. It is timeless and can be transformative if we will only hear and reflect.

The Christmas myth has a powerful contemporary resonance. A couple make an arduous journey to meet the administrative requirements of an occupying power. The woman is pregnant and near her time. There are questions about the paternity of the child but there is also gentle forbearance and care on the part of her husband. They cannot find lodgings and the child is born in a farm shed among dung and straw. A grim experience for them all.

Power is not yet done with this family. The 'star-led wizards' with their curious, unwanted gifts must have been disturbing. More cumber to pack up and carry when all they really need is enough money to find somewhere safe and clean to stay. The puppet-ruler of their colonial masters expected something back from these strange visitors and when he did not get it, became murderous and vengeful on a horrifying scale.

The couple and their new-born child are now refugees, pawns in a hideous power-game. Horrifying rumours of massacre may have reached them as they trekked over 200 miles to take refuge in another country. The very familiarity of the story may cause it to lose impact for us if we respond only to the Christmas card iconography or turn away from the scriptural literalism which insists on an un-nuanced reading.

The true myth is concealed from us by the impossibility of many of the story's appurtenances which some insist we must take literally. The impoverishment is profound and leads us to look for hope in the wrong places. Poverty, vulnerability and violent death are the set in which the circle of eternity and love played out its relationship with the circle of mutability and hatred. "O weary, weary is the world" wrote Chesterton, "but here the world's desire."

A poem by Heather Trickey in this week's issue of the Quaker magazine the Friend catches this for me. It begins "Deck the universal mess in brittle tinsel" and closes "quick now [one small god appears]."

May your small god be with you over these strange days.

A Woman Taken

Across a waterscape full of sky,
waders call from an imagined horizon
where elements may meet.
Here, on a landspit, a man bends
to write in the dust.

Balal's Good Friday
April 18, 2014

Those of us whose trade is words do well to remember the relative value of a picture and a thousand words. The front page of the Guardian yesterday presented an unforgettable instance of the power this adage can carry.

In the first photograph, a young Iranian man stands on the gallows, his mouth wide upon a cry of anguish, his fingers plucking at the noose around his neck. The image of a human being seconds away from death is truly shattering. In the accompanying image, two middle aged women cling to each other and weep.

The young man, named only as Balal, had been condemned to death in northern Iran for killing another youth in a brawl seven years previously. Under the provisions of Sharia law, the family of the victim were to participate in the execution by pulling away the chair on which the condemned man stood. But all did not go as expected. Instead, the mother of the victim stepped forward, slapped Balal's face and then forgave her son's killer. Her husband removed the noose and Balal stepped back from the edge of death. The mothers of victim and killer wept in each other's arms, each in their different ways, transformed and liberated by the act of forgiveness.

This story has been graven into my mind by its associated images. I have always been opposed to the death penalty and have, since childhood, been haunted by the concept of a person knowing the exact moment and place of their death. Judicial killing is a brutal and ultimately futile punishment which rarely satisfies the vengeful impulse for more than a very short space of time, while doubling the devastation of loss and grief.

The grace of the woman who forgave Balal cut through the terror and unavailing rage to give a man back his life. On the eve of the day in which western Christians remember the execution of Jesus, the Poor Man of Nazareth, this immense act of mercy speaks to me of the Divine in the humanity of the wounded and the wounding. The slap is so touchingly human; the refusal to follow through the logic of vengeance is humanity exalted.

May Balal live a good life.

A death in Georgia that diminishes us all
February 16, 2016

In the early hours of 3 February, UK time, the US state of Georgia took the life of Brandon Astor Jones, a 72 year-old African-American.

Brandon Jones committed a crime in 1979 and was in the 37th year of his imprisonment. The details of his offence are easily found online and although it is not certain that he was the 'trigger-man' in the senseless act of violence which ended the life of Roger Tackett, a convenience store cashier, there is no doubt that he was present and was armed.

That act of violence left the family of Mr Tackett a legacy of lifelong grief and trauma. That must not be glossed over or denied. To my knowledge, Brandon never did either of those things.

I speak of knowledge because Brandon and I wrote to each other for many years. Ill-informed assumptions are often made about the nature of relationships between women and the death-row prisoners to whom they write. Let me make clear there was never any question of a romantic or sexual connection in this correspondence. Brandon never wrote to me in a manner which could have been construed as improper or suggestive, nor – contrary to another frequently held belief – did he ever try to get money from me.

Brandon wrote because he loved writing, because he was intelligent and curious and because, as with so many prisoners in his situation, he was hungry for contact, for friendship and for assurance that there was a world beyond his cell which would not abandon him as worthless.

From that tiny cell (approximately six feet by nine and with a cage-style front which permitted no privacy) Brandon corresponded – in the face of difficulties of access to writing materials and postage stamps – with a great many people around the world. He wrote a vast number of essays, many of them published in New Internationalist magazine, and he wrote two books, one of which I edited. His passion for social justice was rooted in his own youthful experience of being a black American at the time of the Civil Rights movement. He was also passionate about equality between women and men and was always eager to hear of the thinking and action of progressives in the UK. His opinions, though firmly held, were not expressed with pomposity or intransigence. Humour and wit frequently came across his pages, despite the absence of the spoken tone.

Brandon was never bitter nor did I ever sense any undertone of violence in his writing although he was frequently angry at the petty tyrannies of prison bureaucracy and the failings of the US penal system. He could be demanding. Editing his book *The Practice of Caring* was not always a smooth ride. All authors are protective of their text and for a man who had so little control over the daily events which most of us take for granted, this was naturally exacerbated. But when I had to explain to him that the demands of my own working life, the transcribing of hand-written chapters and the time scale of the international postal system sometimes acted against the speedy responses he longed for, he was always contrite. This gave me an insight into both the pain of lack of agency and his essential decency. And I will always treasure the gentle and entirely empathetic letter he wrote to me when the time came to have my beloved dog put down. Some may sneer at this from a man who took part in a robbery which ended in the killing of a human being, but I can only say that the man I came to know had travelled a long way from the young criminal who was complicit in that terrible act.

Our worlds and life experiences could hardly have been more different. Despite Brandon's ardent curiosity about the UK, my childhood home, the beliefs of Quakers and above all, the state of politics on this side of the Atlantic, that difference occasionally made us tread carefully with each other. I am aware that no individual can represent their whole racial or demographic group, but I certainly learned a good deal from Brandon about how the world looks to a black American from a background of poverty and disadvantage. It is easy to fall into unconscious assumptions when you are a member of your country's dominant ethnic group. Brandon would never let such assumptions go uncorrected and from him, I gained a deepened understanding of the challenge taken on by declaring oneself to be anti-racist.

Writing to a death row prisoner means living with the ending of that relationship. But this is not about my grief. I write because I must speak to Brandon's humanity and to the long decades lived in the shadow of the execution chamber. These were in some ways his life school and in others, the deforming of his spirit. And above all, I write to tell him and the world that he was "unique, precious, a child of God."

These were also the qualities of Roger Tackett and of Brandon's co-accused, Van Roosevelt Solomon who was executed in 1985. All three lives were taken as the end game of historic failure and dysfunction. The waste is itself criminal. Brandon once wrote to me that he knew "why young black men go wrong". So much of his writing addressed this hard earned knowledge. It was the final failure of the state penal system to lack sufficient vision to see that Brandon had paid his debt by long imprisonment, and to prevent his re-entry into the world he so desired to change.

Instead, they took a 72 year old man in failing health who had spent more than half his life in prison, strapped him to a gurney, inserted a tube in his groin and pumped a drug of unknown provenance into his body. Because reputable pharmaceutical companies will no longer supply execution drugs, these are often impure products, obtained from sources shrouded in secrecy. Brandon did not die quickly or easily.

One day, this will come to an end. My prayer is that through his long imprisonment and ugly judicial killing, Brandon Astor Jones will have played his part in highlighting the obscenity of this 'cruel and unusual punishment' which diminishes us all. May his memory be a blessing.

Finding mercy difficult to stomach
August 24, 2009

On 21 December 1988, I was making a seasonal visit to family in north Cumbria. As we finished our supper and began to clear the table, we heard an explosion and felt a shudder through both air and ground.

Over the next few hours, the terrible facts emerged. A bomb, placed in the baggage hold of Pan Am flight 103, had blown the aircraft out of the sky over the Scottish border town of Lockerbie, raining down debris, fire and death on that small, quiet community. Two hundred and seventy people died as a result of this act of terrorism.

As the magnitude of the catastrophe became clear in the days which followed, a guilty relief merged with my sense of horror. Thirty miles is no distance as a jet airliner flies and had the mid air explosion occurred even a minute earlier, the destruction wrought just across the River Esk could have been visited on any of the villages which lie between Penrith and Carlisle. Our proximity to the disaster has always unnerved me.

It is human nature to feel most acutely that which is nearest and Lockerbie has troubled my dreams many times during the last 20 years. But that is as nothing to the ongoing suffering of the families to whom death came so suddenly and with such appalling violence on that winter night.

It was with some sense of relief, therefore that the world heard, 13 years later, of the conviction of the Libyan intelligence officer, Abdelbaset Ali al-Megrahi, for his part in this act of terrorism. A specially convened court of three Scottish judges sitting in the Hague sentenced al-Megrahi to life imprisonment with a minimum tariff of 27 years.

Although it was evident that he could not have acted alone, there was a feeling that justice had been done and reparation would, in some part, be made.

Now, eight years into his sentence and terminally ill, al-Megrahi has been released so he may return to Libya and die with his family around him. There has been a huge outcry at this act of mercy on the part of the Scottish government.

The pain of the bereaved, the fact that al-Megrahi denied his victims the love-supported death now granted to him, the gloating exhibitionism of his reception in Libya and the possibilities of a trade deal having been done for the benefit of the UK, have all been cited in opposition to his release. There may be substance in all these arguments. But none of them take cognisance of the unique quality of mercy.

Mercy cannot be earned, it is never deserved (if it were, it would not be mercy) and it is not a *quid pro quo*. It is pure gift and whenever we exercise it, we come closer to the Divine nature.

In contradicting our instinct for revenge – itself a perversion of true justice – it challenges our society's spiritual illiteracy and our consequent inability to comprehend that what is right may be costly, not to our apparent advantage and at odds with worldly 'realism'.

The statement made by the Scottish Justice Minister, Kenny MacAskill, may have tended towards the dramatic and many have criticised him for making reference to a "higher power".

But his words have a quality which has the capacity to raise our eyes to a truth above realpolitik. Reminding us that death is universal and non-negotiable and that the good society must operate on principle as well as pragmatism, the passage concerned is worth reading again: "Mr al-Megrahi faces a sentence imposed by a higher power. It is one that no court, in any jurisdiction, in any land, could revoke or overrule...Our justice system demands that judgement be imposed but compassion be available. Our beliefs dictate that justice be served but mercy be shown."

Our culture finds the concept of compassion easier than that of mercy. They are related but not indivisible virtues. One may find it hard to feel compassion for al-Megrahi whilst still believing that he should be shown mercy. Compassion makes a claim on emotion, mercy on something sterner.

I have returned many times to the Sermon on the Mount whilst thinking about this article: "Blessed are the merciful, for they will be shown mercy". These words of Jesus are so familiar that there is a danger of overlooking their transformative power. If we do not know the nature of mercy, it will not grow amongst us. And what is not known, can be neither practised nor received.

Mercy reflects God to us in a unique manner. It invites us to share in the wholeness for which we were created. If we permit ourselves to become caught up in the power games between Holyrood, Westminster, Washington and Tripoli, we will miss the truth.

Suburban Regret

They are moving, the family across the way.
We are not sorry: he was so difficult about the parking,
her apology a sidle-glancing, anxious smile.

The children, always unspeaking, grew taller and pale.
They seemed wakelights waiting flame.
I wish we had done better.

Moving beyond unexamined outrage
August 11, 2009

Last week, a woman asked a group of youths in a Leeds cinema to make less noise. Today, it is still uncertain as to whether her sight will be permanently damaged following their vicious retaliation, for which a sixteen year-old boy is now in custody. The woman had taken her two children to a screening of Harry Potter and the Half Blood Prince, but their enjoyment of this holiday treat was marred by the rowdiness of the youths. Resentful at being asked to modify their behaviour, the offenders followed the family to a restaurant and threw bleach in the woman's face.

I will admit to a *Daily Mail* moment when I heard of this barbarous action. The phrases 'lock them up and throw away the key' and 'broken Britain' flashed across my mental screen until the responsibility of subjecting emotional reaction to reasoned analysis reasserted itself.

This was an appalling act of violence. Some form of punishment, reparation and reformation must follow. But nothing is without cause and actions do not take place within a vacuum. Seeking to understand what might lie behind this attack, I asked a consultant psychiatrist for his view.

"Young males are the among the most psychologically vulnerable members of society", he told me. He explained that they are the most likely to be subject to attention deficiency disorders, to impulsive action and risk taking and are more readily influenced by peer pressure than any other social grouping.

The consequent conduct disorder from which many of them suffer and which so frequently manifests in anti-social behaviour, often continues into later life unless it is correctly managed and may decline into a persistent personality disorder. Our prisons are over-populated by individuals suffering from such disorders.

This intrinsic vulnerability in the young male places a considerable responsibility on society as a whole. Where parenting is poor, the responsibility becomes even greater and the window of opportunity is alarmingly narrow. A primary school head, reinforcing the Jesuit maxim "give me a boy till he is seven and I will give you the man", told me that by the age of eight or nine "there is only remedial action".

For many years I have been writing to a Death Row prisoner in the United States. Because he asked me not to name him before his execution, I will call him Ben. As with the majority of such prisoners he is black, poorly educated and from a heartbreakingly dysfunctional family.

Born before the Civil Rights movement began to ameliorate some of the indignities and injustices experienced by black Americans, Ben's early experiences of prejudice and discrimination deformed his emerging character. He ran away from home at the age of 11 and thereafter lived by his wits.

It would have been a miracle had he not drifted into crime. Almost 35 years ago, he took part in an armed robbery during which a shop assistant was shot dead. Though Ben's was not the finger on the trigger, the Law of Parties obtaining in the state where the crime was committed, meant that he too received the death penalty.

Now in his sixties, Ben is a thoughtful and morally mature man. He has become widely read and takes a keen interest in social and political thinking. Recently he wrote to me on the subject of youth violence and anti-social behaviour.

These words from the shadow of the execution chamber demand our attention. "We need to teach anger-management and conflict resolution as soon as we start teaching the ABC". Believing that we must equip children to handle rejection and frustration without resorting to violence, he urges "an incremental upgrade of these skills all the way through college." If this were to be done, Ben predicts the result would be "a reduction in husbands killing their wives, students terrorising their campuses and less blood on the surface of every school-yard."

This wisdom has been hard-earned and his closing words are particularly poignant: "Unfortunately, no-one wants to hear from the likes of me."

But it is exactly the likes of Ben to whom we should be listening. His life experience makes him a prophetic voice. He has lived with the consequences of parental failure and knows that there has to be a wider responsibility for in creating the civilising and graceful disciplines which build up human dignity and make it possible for society to cohere. If these are neglected, the social and personal frailties of the young, and of young men in particular, will continue to manifest in destructive behaviour.

The sensibilities which enable us to take up these responsibilities are being eroded. Aggressive language is frequently the default reaction to relatively minor irritations. It is too often heard in the media and in entertainment because to be thought 'edgy' is a money spinner.

A more accurate description of this style of speech and behaviour would be "immature and degenerate." Last summer, Top Gear presenter Jeremy Clarkson, a man for whom puerile irresponsibility is a profitable brand, told an audience at the Hay Literary Festival that people who are late for appointments "should be shot in the face".

That ugly and intemperate remark reveals the persistence of the petulant toddler in the adult. That we pay for and consume it without protest is to our shame. Highly paid middle-aged toddlers, misogynist rappers, and foul-mouthed celebrity presenters all contribute to a coarsening of the grain of our common life. There should be no place of neutrality when we are faced with this kind of normalisation of the cruel and self-indulgent.

More is demanded of us. When 16 year old Jimmy Mizen was stabbed to death in a London café in 2008, his grieving father reminded us of our collective duty to "look at ourselves and the values we would like". The values we are willing to tolerate and those we would like, need to be brought closer together. Doing so requires constant examination of our own attitudes and responses. Every time we fail in showing our children how to deal with life's inevitable disappointments and obstacles, we set them up for adverse reactions in later years.

The frustrated toddler, throwing itself on the ground in a passion of tears, does so because it has not yet learned that its desires are not the only show in town. Guidance and example in developing self-control in the formative years is essential to moral self-management in maturity. Every time we permit ourselves to lash out verbally when thwarted or disappointed, we do not simply display a lack of restraint, we become complicit in a growing culture of aggression.

Politicians vie with each other to appear tough on crime. Tabloid papers crusade for longer sentences to already overcrowded and dysfunctional prisons. In doing so, they plug into reactive moments of horror and anger such as that which I experienced on hearing of the attack in Leeds. If those moments go unchallenged and are permitted to coalesce into a world-view, we will continue to fail in our collective responsibility for our most disturbed young people.

The quaintly named *Advices and Queries*, a collection of questions and challenges designed to help Quakers in the everyday practise of their beliefs, offers us this: "Bring into God's light those emotions, attitudes and prejudices in yourself which lie at the root of destructive conflict, acknowledging your need for forgiveness and grace." If we cannot do this, it is unlikely that we will be able to answer the subsequent question,"In what ways are you involved in the work of reconciliation between individuals, groups and nations?"

There is too much at stake, both in ruined lives and in the fragmenting of society, to permit the option of a retreat into unexamined outrage.

Wise monkeys or vicious beasts? Abuse, cruelty and free speech
August 10, 2013

Our animal natures are in a constant state of tension between the personal and the communal. We have instincts which drive us to gratify ourselves, to dominate in pursuit of food, status and mates. And then we have the pull towards the good of the tribe, pack or troop and the protection and support it offers.

This is not to place biological determinism ahead of the qualities of grace and civilisation which human kind has acquired over millennia of evolution. But it maybe does no harm to remind ourselves of our primate characteristics. Know your opponent is a wise strategy.

The news that another young teenager had taken their life after abuse and bullying on a social networking site this week should bring us up short. It is impossible to truly imagine the anguish of 14 year old Hannah Smith in the days that led up to her death, nor the pain of her family both now, and in the years to come.

It is a simple fact of biology that the human brain is not fully developed until the third decade of life. Adolescents do not make the same connections as adults, nor do they have the capacity to weigh, balance, discern and make the choices that are possible for the mature neural network. This is one of the reasons that they have a claim on our protection, forbearance and example.

The recent abuse and threats of violence visited on women commentators and campaigners via the medium of Twitter are the vicious outpourings of immature and unregulated minds. Where they threaten violence, they are criminal acts and must be dealt with accordingly. My wholehearted sympathies are with Caroline Criado Perez, Mary Beard and Stella Creasy. I received a couple of nasty comments last week but they consisted of puerile obscenities rather that threats of rape or murder. Unpleasant, but one blocks and moves on, grateful for the support of those who speak up in condemnation and defence.

But these are acts on a spectrum of disorder and unkindness that should concern us all because they affect us all. They also have their roots in the kind of society we are willing to be. Speaking earlier this week on BBC Radio 4's Thought for the Day, Rabbi Jonathan Sacks spoke of what is known in Judaism as 'Lashon Hara' or 'evil speech'. Its practice, he said, destroys the one who utters the words, the one who receives them, and those who listen in.

None of us are exempt from that last category. What are we willing to accept in our daily lives? How do we respond when we are frustrated or find ourselves in disagreement? Should we tut up our sleeves when we overhear cruel or intemperate words instead of challenging them? What will we permit to become the norm?

Free speech is not speech which costs nothing, the Chief Rabbi reminded us. There is a huge cost in cruelty and distress if we become too apathetic or too craven to stand up against the coarsening of our human and social grain.

It is not sufficient to leave all the responsibility with the social networking sites. They can do better, but so can we all. Our young people will model what they see and hear. Shall we be wise monkeys or vicious beasts?

Two Nations

"Two nations; between whom there is no intercourse and no sympathy; who are as ignorant of each other's habits, thoughts, and feelings, as if they were dwellers in different zones, or inhabitants of different planets" – Benjamin Disraeli

Your eyes sidle across us.
You note our poor complexions, faces scored with strain,
the cheap clothes and tattered plastic bags.

You hurry past our unknown streets.
Daily we map the trails you abjure: our eastings are
drawn on other axes.

We are threaded on the strings of your disquiet:
amulets of unease, the death's head graved on your plenty.
We keep your distance.

Poverty and hope abandoned: learning again the spiritual value of each other

May 25, 2015

Lasciate ogne speranza, voi ch'intrate (Abandon all hope, ye who enter here). The words Dante places over the gates of hell are terrifying. And to turn that cause and effect around is to remind ourselves of the devastation wrought in lives where hope has gone.

Most of us will have had very dark times in our lives. I count myself fortunate that even at my lowest, I have never quite ceased to hope for hope, to believe in the possibility that things would not always be this way. Maybe this is partly genetics, but most likely it is informed by a secure childhood, loving relationships and the experience that hard work, prudence and endurance would eventually get me to a better place. In other words, I belong to the lucky sperm club.

But real poverty is another country. The experiences are different there. Deprivation is not just about having insufficient money, crushing though that is – it is an accumulation of the malign influences which hover around the cradle of a child born into family dysfunction in decaying locations where angry and brutish behaviours deform the environment and suck the confidence out of all but the most ruthless.

Depressed, struggling parents – often in precarious relationships – do not raise happy and well-adjusted children. Listen to the flat, expressionless speech of a person who has experienced emotional abuse from damaged parents, and do not raise a disapproving eyebrow when discovering that they go on to make poor life choices. Ill health, both mental and physical, is of course, found across all socio-economic groups, but both its prevalence and impact are disproportionate where people live in poverty.

Because when you are ill, depressed, unable to work, harried and sanctioned by a benefit regime which believes you need to be punished into conformity with its ideal, fear, hunger and cold are added to your burdens. There is no respite, no monetary remedy. You can't afford to go anywhere. You have no friends. You are unable to engage with society. You have become *de facto* a pariah, experiencing the isolation which is one of the most destructive conditions for the human spirit.

Our policy makers and legislators are higher rate tax payers. They mix with others of the same kind because that is what most of us do for most of the time. They theorise about deprivation and their place on the political spectrum determines the level of indifference and contempt displayed towards those they find unattractive. That attitude has enabled the appallingly negative stereotypes of poverty which are the staple of media portrayals such as Benefits Street. It stirs up hate-filled comment in the press and on social media. It drives the already desperate still nearer to the edge.

While politicians compete with each other to sell themselves as the parties of 'aspiration', can we remain silent about what is being done to so many abandoned, hopeless people? Must we not challenge a concept of aspiring which is more about consumerism than humane and sustainable betterment?

In 1987, Quakers in Britain issued a declaration ahead of the General Election which returned Margaret Thatcher to her third term in government. It contained these words: "We commit ourselves to learning again the spiritual value of each other. We find ourselves utterly at odds with the priorities in our society which deny the full human potential of millions of people in this country. That denial diminishes us all. There must be no 'them' and 'us'".

So if you watch Benefits Street tonight, take a step for those values by sharing the reality which does not tickle the fancies of the contemptuous. Urge your MP to reconsider indifference or hostility towards people they cannot be bothered to understand or of whose experience they are content to remain ignorant.

Challenge them to spend some time in talking to people they would rather not meet. Dare them to leave behind their preconceptions and ideological remedies. Insist that they do this without an eye for publicity but with a heart for making real connections. Demand the humility and perseverance that could begin to build the relational structures which make it possible to rediscover the spiritual value of people who have no hope.

Inequality 1987–2015: what has changed and what must never change
March 17, 2015

Sometimes it seems as though nothing much changes. In 1987, London Yearly Meeting of the Religious Society of Friends issued a public statement in the month before the General Election of that year. It expressed anger at the polarisation of the country; condemned inequality and expressed Quakers' belief that urgent action was needed to "promote debate and to stimulate action".

During the period 6-15 March 2015, Friends across Britain have been taking action for Quaker Equality Week. Over 80 Local Meetings have held vigils, exhibitions, debates, shown films and invited engagement from election candidates. Looking at my own Meeting, I am heartened by the media coverage we have received and the good reception from the local community.

So should we feel downcast that on one hand, so much of what was highlighted almost 30 years ago is still with us – and is arguably getting worse – or are there signs of change? Let's look at that statement from a generation ago in a little more detail.

"We are angered by actions which have knowingly led to the polarisation of our country – into the affluent, who epitomise success according to the values of a materialistic society, and the 'have-leasts', who by the expectations of that same society are oppressed, judged, found wanting and punished. "

This was the 'loadsamoney' era. We were invited to believe that greed was good and our government was led by a Prime Minister to whom the phrase "A man who, beyond the age of 26, finds himself on a bus can count himself as a failure" was attributed. It is only fair to say that this has never been verified, but it is significant that no one from her government rushed to deny the attribution. It fitted well with the contemporary growth in individualism, taking in casual sexism and contempt for public services along the way.

The emphasis here was on success measured in monetary terms, and on worth as concomitant with acquisition. The obvious outcome was an oppressive judgement of those who did not manifest the outward appearances of 'success', whether through choice, incapacity or lack of realistic opportunity. There has been some muting of the yuppie braying of that period and although the red braces and wine bar excesses may largely have disappeared, inequalities of wealth in 2015 are greater than ever.

The punitive element referred to the 1987 statement has increased to a dangerous level. Divisive language about 'scroungers' and 'skivers' is doing untold damage to our social cohesion and the arbitrary application of sanctions to benefit recipients has normalised the notion that to be in need is evidence of a feckless inadequacy, requiring chastisement by the more fortunate.

Whatever government ministers may claim about this 'helping' people back into work, there is no escaping the intent to punish. Indeed, that very intent was made clear in Channel 4's recent Dispatches: Benefits Britain, when a Job Centre Advisor was filmed telling an undercover reporter posing as a trainee: "The whole idea is the punishment, that's what you've got to suffer." This is cruel and unjust. There can be no condition of employment in which being five minutes late or getting something wrong due to a superior's administrative error could result in disciplinary action reducing its recipient to destitution and hunger. There were very few food banks in 1987.

"As a Religious Society and as individuals we commit ourselves to examine again how we use our personal and financial resources. We will press for change to enable wealth and power to be shared more evenly within our nation. We make this statement publicly at a time of national decision [a general election] in the hope that, following the leadings of the Spirit, each one of us in Britain will take appropriate action."

The capacity to take appropriate action is the point at which hope becomes visible. Although the conditions of 1987 appear little changed, there is one large and significant difference. It is the internet. Thirty years ago, communication and the sharing of knowledge was very different. It was difficult to get information and even more difficult to combine quickly and effectively with others in taking action. Social media, blogs and websites now make it easy for groups and individuals to raise awareness, share ideas and make matters uncomfortable for politicians who would otherwise thrive on unexamined falsehood and the electorate's ignorance of facts. The examination of personal and financial resources in the internet age has given rise to effective combined action and a wider knowledge of unjust conditions. This is a significant and welcome change.

"We value that of God in each person, and affirm the right of everyone to contribute to society and share in life's good things, beyond the basic necessities. We commit ourselves to learning again the spiritual value of each other. We find ourselves utterly at odds with the priorities in our society which deny the full human potential of millions of people in this country. That denial diminishes us all. There must be no 'them' and 'us' ". That has not changed. It must never change.

How the poor die – and how power must learn from their lives
July 11, 2017

In 1929, George Orwell was admitted to a public hospital in Paris. He was suffering from pneumonia and spent several weeks as a non-paying patient in the Hôpital Cochin. The essay he wrote about this experience remained unpublished for almost two decades, only appearing in *Now*, a political and literary magazine published by the writer and critic George Woodcock in 1946.

It is not difficult to see why such a distressing and disturbing piece of first hand experience would have been thought a risky bet amongst editors reluctant to harrow their readers: "In the public wards of a hospital you see horrors that you don't seem to meet with among people who manage to die in their own homes, as though certain diseases only attacked people at the lower income levels...This business of people just dying like animals, for instance, with nobody standing by, nobody interested, the death not even noticed till the morning – this happened more than once."

This was, of course, almost 90 years ago. Although *How the Poor Die* details medically crude procedures which are long gone, Orwell's essay still has something to tell us about an attitude towards the provision of what is no more than minimally acceptable – if that – for people who are without money or influence.

The terrible deaths at Grenfell Tower tell the same story. From inferior quality building materials, lack of safety equipment and poor inspection regimes, to the inadequacy displayed by the Royal Borough of Kensington and Chelsea and the Prime Minister, the narrative is one of neglectful contempt for the public realm. It is impossible to believe that residents of an 'exclusive development' would have had the same experiences.

But one thing has changed beyond measure since Orwell recorded the appalling treatment of patients in Hôpital Cochin, and that is the almost immediate visibility of the suffering and the unfolding sequence of dysfunction and incomprehension in the days following 14 June. Whereas *How the Poor Die* reached only the readers of a small left-wing magazine, the horror that is Grenfell has not only been seen all around the world, but the survivors and their supporters, through their social media presence and effectiveness in organising, have spoken with a voice that cannot be ignored.

For the first time that I can recall, the rulers have had to face the ruled in uncontrolled circumstances under the eye of the world's media. They handled this with varying degrees of incompetence and there are signs that they are already trying to re-bottle the genie. But both the human qualities and the realities of life for the just-about-surviving have been laid inescapably before a power which has hitherto preferred not to look too closely.

A disabled man lived and died on the 21st floor of Grenfell Tower. Families were bringing up children six stories and more above the ground. No one appears to know just how many lived in the tower because some flats were sublet and some tenants would seem to have been undocumented migrants. 'Unofficial' lives are not necessarily evidence of innate criminality or fecklessness: people learn to go below the radar when an environment is hostile to their existences.

As widely separated cultures were forced into proximity, the most telling moment for me came when Andrea Leadsom, Leader of the House of Commons, visited the site and was approached by a group of five or six residents. They were polite but searching in their questions and challenging as to why council officials had been invisible in the aftermath of the fire. The questioning was led by a young man who did not speak in Received Pronunciation. He was articulate and persistent without becoming aggressive and his poise and moral intelligence were very obviously unsettling to Ms Leadsom. She deserves credit for being available to such questioning – a stance which her leader had been unable to take – but it was both comical and disturbing to watch her struggling to recalibrate her preconceptions even as they were in the process of being overset.

This must be the lasting legacy of Grenfell. If we are to move towards a more equal, just and empathetic society, the assumptions of superiority which flourish in privileged isolation cannot continue. The rolling-back and de-regulation of the state, with its disproportionate effect on the most vulnerable, has come under scrutiny and the lives of people who too often go unnoticed have been seen in every sitting room in the country. Those who hold power and those who make and execute policy must not be permitted to forget.

Hidden

Sometimes, I wonder at hidden lives.
They seem as a pale owl,
caught at moth-light in the eye's tail;
the old man silent on a park bench
and the blank-faced child in a ruined street.

Many the faces and forms of all that live.
Their ways, words and cries
lie along unknown paths,
but keep alive a questioning heart.

Our calloused hearts and people of unnoticed lives
February 14, 2017

"People of unnoticed lives. " These words leaped out of the radio for me last week when BBC Radio 4's 'Aftermath' revisited the deaths of 23 Chinese cockle-pickers on the sands of Morecambe Bay in 2004.

Those horrible deaths have been described as the "dark underbelly of globalisation". This is true. Paid far less than the going rate for local workers, these men and women had been illegally brought into the UK in shipping containers by a combination of Chinese Triads and UK gangmasters. Things have changed in the intervening 13 years – the exploitation of these desperate, vulnerable people was a direct cause of the establishment of the Gangmaster Licensing Authority and its legislation for the protection and reform of moral and legal standards.

This knowledge also calls to us to reflect on the immense gulf of perception between that which we know and that which is the reality of experience for so many. At the risk of coming close to the 'known un-knowns' of Donald Rumsfeld territory, it should be remembered that to notice is the beginning of knowledge, and knowledge, the beginning of empathy. To be content in not noticing, is to will isolation and moral deformation.

Most of us would never have noticed the Chinese cockle-pickers had their handlers not been ignorant of local tides which sweep in faster than a man can run. These were disposable people in the think-ing of those who had power over them and who believed they could stay beneath our moral radar. We are more aware now and, in an in-terconnected world, have fewer excuses for remaining unsighted. But too many lives still remain hidden in plain view because we tend to live in silos of comfort, ethnicity, religion and fear. It is perhaps, economic status which most divides us. If you have a reasonable disposable in-come, live in a pleasant neighbourhood and feel fairly secure in your job, what do you see of the insecurely employed and housed, the food bank user or the zero hours worker struggling to manage rent, utilities and children's shoes? You may read about them, but you don't look in their eyes and hear their experiences. Prosperity prefers to keep the disquieting at arms length.

It becomes easier to attribute fault and failure to those whose lives are not like our own if we do not see them in a physical sense. Our common humanity is not acknowledged and understanding is unlikely to be enlarged. If the just-about-managing, the not-managing-at-all, the migrant worker, the asylum seeker and the Muslim are not sharing our space, we are not encountering their experiences. Stereotyping has free rein and a malign feedback loop is created which makes true encounter ever more unlikely.

It is, of course, easier to identify a problem than to find solutions. But if equality and justice are to mean anything, they must challenge us to self-examination. A wave of nationalism and racism is rising in Europe. The weirding of American politics is unsettling societies throughout the world. Our own politics is increasingly being evacuated of vision, altruism, compassion and truthfulness. There is an urgent need to begin the building of moral communities. And if that is to happen, we must notice each other across boundaries of location, economic status, race, faith and party. It has been said: "For this people's heart has become calloused; they hardly hear with their ears, and they have closed their eyes." In the just society no one is invisible, no one can be disposable.

Rowan Williams on food banks, truth and solidarity
March 13, 2014

A couple of days ago, I sat in a packed church in a Cambridgeshire village to hear Rowan Williams speak about food banks. The former Archbishop of Canterbury was measured and carefully non-party political in his observations. His address was a model of the power which is exercised when discernment is coupled with commitment to truth and justice.

Dr Williams is a patron of Cambridge City Food Bank and he evidently does far more than lend his name to its work A central theme of his discourse was the immense value of listening to and respecting the experience of food bank users and thus restoring some sense of dignity and worth to those whom the current political culture seeks to abase and demonise.

Speaking of the Christian belief in a God who has "a particular concern for those everyone else wants to forget; those who rarely break the surface", he reminded his audience that to sit and listen is of equal importance with the provision of food. He described many of those with whom he speaks as "feeling humiliated, feeling that they've let down their families. They need us to work with the grain of their dignity."

That refusal to follow the facile populist indignation so carefully fostered by the government and some of its media allies is a sign of authentic discipleship. Rowan Williams has probably not experienced much financial hardship in his life. He held the highest office of the Established Church and is now Master of a Cambridge college. But as a man who evidently waits attentively upon the Spirit, he has understood and internalised the manner in which a cascade of relatively small financial difficulties may so terrifyingly combine to bring the 'precariat' to the edge of destitution. The comfortable should heed him.

Along with his conviction that the followers of Jesus are called to solidarity with the vulnerable and suffering, Rowan Williams also challenges power to put truth ahead of expediency. He castigated politicians for their reluctance to visit food banks and put their preconceptions to the test: "I haven't been struck by their willingness to take up invitations". He condemned those who "pretend that the need is not real" and who "for reasons of ideology and comfort" will not accept what may be inconvenient to their beliefs. He insisted that it is essential to admit "there is a cost" to the policies being pursued and to acknowledge that this must be documented with integrity and kept under review if we are to find a better way forward.

What difference can we make? This is the challenge Rowan Williams laid down on a chilly March evening in a Fen-edge church. Not just to politicians but to every single one of us.

War, peace and memory

Lyness Naval Cemetery 2016

A century gone. This wind bared place once framed sharper grief.
The salt cold bodies newly graved;
homes without boys' laughter;
the end of meaning.

Bands, politicians, dress uniforms and solemn words:
these the tools of management.
Assembling heroes from terrified children because
heroes are safe.

Jutland. A heading in history.
Have mercy on us.

Remembering well: poetry, pity and truth
November 18, 2016

The 2016 season of remembrance is over. But the challenge of how to re-
member well never leaves us.

The annual disagreements about poppy colour and indeed, about the
pressure to wear a poppy of any hue, are done for a while and having
kept my written and broadcast contributions on the topic to a minimum
this year, I have found a spiritual space in which to reflect upon what the
Quaker Testimony to Truth asks of us in relation to remembrance.

Wilfred Owen's words: "My subject is War, and the pity of War. The
Poetry is in the pity" are well known, and together with silence – its close
kin – poetry has guided me to a necessary place of discomfort this year.

It is the instinct of most people to attempt to comfort the anguished.
But can that be done by drawing on falsehood? How far may we justifiably
go in shielding the bereaved from reality or in helping them to construct a
shelter built on sand? Siegfried Sassoon's poem 'The Hero' began to nag at
my conscience when I first read it as a teenager. The pain does not dimin-
ish as maturity brings a deeper experience of suffering.

> 'Jack fell as he'd have wished,' the mother said,
> And folded up the letter that she'd read.
> 'The Colonel writes so nicely.' Something broke
> In the tired voice that quavered to a choke.
> She half looked up. 'We mothers are so proud
> Of our dead soldiers.' Then her face was bowed.

The real circumstances of Jack's death are concealed by the officer who
visits the bereaved mother and the compassion exercised is probably the
line most of us would choose to take. But if compassion as 'suffering with'
is to be honoured, we need to be sufficiently stern with ourselves to re-
alise both the futility of violence and the pull towards creating ways of
thinking that will protect us from facing that abyss of meaninglessness.
Once again, it is poetry which cleanses the perception, acknowledging our
frailty whilst reminding us of its capacity to delude:

> ...human kind
> Cannot bear very much reality.

This is not just about the physical horrors of violent death. The
grieving mother in Sassoon's poem needed to sustain a vision of her
son's death as something sanctified by high purpose. So much of the

language of remembrance is wrought to this end. The 'giving' of lives; the ennobling 'sacrifice'; the 'growing not old'. War is failure. It is the failure of politics, of diplomacy, of vision, of "man as a thinking animal", in John Steinbeck's powerful phrase. And the price of that failure is paid by the combatants who did not grow old because their elders made of them a sacrifice. They did not 'give' their lives, they were robbed of them, in their youth and their valour. We find the reality unconscionable and seek our sanity in platitude – the 'old lie' of Wilfred Owen's *Dulce et Decorum Est*.

How are we to deal with this? Who would want to twist the blade in the unimaginable wound? I bring a question, not as yet an answer. But in the silence of Meeting for Worship on Remembrance Sunday, I found a way-post: the Testimony to Peace and the Testimony to Truth are inextricable. Liturgies and rites of remembrance are shaped to draw us away from those desolate landscapes where truth seems too dangerous to be faced – an existential threat which may bring us crashing down in grief and despair. However solemn, well-crafted and impressively executed the familiar rituals may be, they are in danger of being the enemy of peace so long as they serve to gloss the failure and utter waste of war.

On the afternoon of Remembrance Sunday, our Meeting laid a wreath of white poppies at the town's war memorial. The military ceremonial had long finished and the streets were quiet as around 30 of us gathered to read short quotations on peace and the making of peace before remaining a while in silence. Without the displacement activity of pageantry, martial music and uniformed spectacle, we could only stand with our own sorrow and penitence. It is a hard place to inhabit but it is perhaps where we may begin to learn how to remember with honesty and therefore with hope for a better future.

Remember: *Young Soldier* by Wilfred Owen, killed in action one week before the Armistice of 1918:

> It is the smile
> Faint as a (waning) myth,
> Faint, and exceeding small
> On a boy's murdered mouth.

Remember: the words of a great poet of our own time. Geoffrey Hill, who died only a few weeks ago:

> ...a nation with so many memorials but no memory.

The uses of memory: looking beyond chocolate bars
November 18, 2014

The Blood Swept Land and Seas of Red installation is gone from the Tower of London. The disputes over white poppies and the British Legion's misuse of Eric Bogle's 'Green Fields of France' have died away. But in this centenary year of the start of the first World War, there is much remembering – both honest and contrived – still to be done.

Never overestimate the crassness quotient of advertising. With an eye to both the Christmas market and the sentiment aroused by the official rites of remembrance-tide, Sainsbury's Christmas commercial plumbed new depths of both sentimentality and cynicism.

The historic 1914 Christmas truce and game of football in No-Man's Land was turned into a two-minute tear-jerker which culminates in a British Tommy slipping a chocolate bar into the pocket of a young German soldier before the monstrous anger of the guns began again. Sainsbury's were reported to be selling 5000 replicas of that chocolate bar per hour last week.

The advert has so far received more than 8 million hits on YouTube and has been variously described as "a masterpiece", "grim", "epic", and "disrespectful". That half the profits are destined for the Royal British Legion does no credit to that organisation nor does it redeem the use of the pity and horror of war to sell confectionery.

There is a strange 'emotion at a remove' aspect to much of this year's memorialising which reminds me a little of the curious phenomenon which overtook much of Britain in August 1997.

We were in London during that weekend in which the life of Diana, Princess of Wales was cut so short in a Paris underpass. At first, the people we met in the newsagent's or taking Sunday strolls in the park were expressing genuine sadness and shock at so untimely a death. It was only as the day wore on that the extravagant carpet of flowers began to appear. In the days which followed, the nation plunged into an orgy of grief which many of us found disturbing. I shall not forget a tear-stained woman telling the cameras that she had not grieved like this for her own mother. There was something about the flood of emotion which seemed to have little time for reticence and none at all for questioning.

Although on a lesser scale, the Tower of London display appears to touch a similar nerve. From Nigel Farage's tearful display (derided by all who observed it) to the interviews with people grieving the great-grandfathers they had never known, something rings, if not a little false, rather close to the temporary and superficial. The carnage, the brutality, the shot-at-dawn terrified and traumatised teenagers, the ruined and haunted generation – all these demand something quieter, less showy and, perhaps, more analytical if we are to honour those on all sides whose lives were taken from them under circumstances of immense folly and futility.

"This is the use of memory: for liberation" wrote TS Eliot. If the fashion in remembrance stops at stimulating the kind of emotion that is here today and gone tomorrow – even if sustained by feel-good purchasing – we shall be less inclined to go on the difficult journey of metanoia and re-making which war and the ending of war requires of us and in which lies the ultimate liberation of humanity.

Truth, lies and the pain of remembrance
November 9, 2010

Wilfred Owen's poem 'Dulce et Decorum est' entered my conscious-ness around the time I began to learn Latin. The soldier-poet's horrify-ing description of the terror of men experiencing a gas attack and de-tails of the suffering endured by those who did not get their masks on in time, forms a powerful disjunction with the quotation from Horace – *Dulce et decorum est pro patria mori* – it is sweet and fitting to die for your country.

My child's mind had begun to perceive Latin as the language of tra-dition and dignity and my willingness to receive its music as transmit-ting something of great portent received a jolt from this poem. I began to wonder then at the language we use for memorialising and have continued to do so for over 40 years.

At this time of the year, there is no escaping the difficulty. Last week I stood in front of a war memorial in a small market town and looked at the inscription 'Our glorious dead' followed by the admonition 'see to it that they are not forgotten'.

The old shock from that long ago English Literature lesson returned. Why are these young men whose lives were taken so brutally, 'glori-ous'? And what are we to make of the slightly bossy warning which followed? What must we do to grasp the meaning, to remember their suffering and grasp the human dignity lying so far beyond the ritual words of remembrance?

A group of veterans who fought in Northern Ireland and the Falklands wrote to the Guardian newspaper last week to challenge the accepted language of remembrance and its outcomes.

Challenging the "showbiz hype" of the campaign to "wear a poppy in support of 'our heroes'" they point out that there is nothing heroic about being blown up or shot in an unnecessary war. It is only the fact that the writers are men who have lived this reality which prevents widespread howls of rage from the armchair green-berets.

For most of my life, remembrance has been focused on the two world wars of the 20th century. Now, with the conflict in Afghanistan sending young men home maimed or in coffins, we are dealing with something contemporary, something which spreads its tentacles of grief and loss into our own towns and workplaces.

We have to learn to speak truth to unimaginable suffering without ever forgetting the truncated lives of so many young soldiers and the lifelong pain of their families. We have to find the words, now, today.

We are paralysed before the anguish of parents whose life sentence it is to imagine their son screaming in fear and pain during the last minutes of his life. We are left dumb in the presence of a young mother whose baby will never know its father. So, casting around for something – anything – that may offer comfort, we plug into the rhetorical devices of remembrance.

But listen again to Owen. The terrified men, the bleak facts of mortal wounds – "if you could hear at every jolt, the blood come gargling from the froth-corrupted lungs", the hopelessness of young men whose lives are all but over – "his hanging face, like a devil's sick of sin".

How are we to bear what he puts before us? Only by facing the truth. Only by accepting that this is not glorious, that it is the vile outcome of failure by politicians, rulers, generals – by all of us who acquiesce in the delusion of glory and heroism, who are ready to confuse care for 'our boys' with anything other than peacemaking.

Only then might we begin to remember with integrity and accept that there is no inherent virtue in ceremony and no lasting consolation in high-flown periods or patriotic clichés.

Wilfred Owen had the right to rail against "the old lie" He survived all the horrors of trench warfare only to be killed by a sniper on the day peace was declared.

I was not there and so you may sneer at what I have to say. But I am the daughter and granddaughter of men who were, in their different ways, broken by war. They were determined that we, the young ones, should not "be ardent for some desperate glory". We must not let them down.

On Armed Forces Day

Peace wears plain dress, without gaud to attract the fickle eye.
There is no shoring strut, no diversion to easeful pride.
It gathers among lives, as seed cases in paving cracks, then blows.
But one dustgold germ may root, one ending begin behind
the blare of bands.

Armed Forces Day and the quieter voice
June 26, 2017

It seems that just as 'poppy fascism' is beginning to lose its sway over our consciences and behaviours, Armed Forces Day is being groomed to take its place.

Jeremy Corbyn has been criticised in some quarters for accepting a long-standing invitation to Glastonbury rather than attending an Armed Forces Day event. James Heappey, the MP for Wells, wrote a letter to Corbyn inviting him to a parade in Burnham-on-Sea, just ten hours ahead of the occasion. That the communication of useful information was not the primary purpose of this missive would seem to be confirmed by Heappey's publication of the letter on social media. At the best, this could be perceived as a failure of good manners.

Then there was the irritably-toned Twitter response from a retired army officer to this statement from Jeremy Corbyn: "On Armed Forces Day, I thank our dedicated forces and veterans for their service, sacrifice and commitment". This apparently, showed "utter disrespect" because "Corbyn doesn't know the difference between Armed Forces Day and Remembrance Sunday. Thinks they're interchangeable". It seems that this very similar contribution from the Defence Secretary, Michael Fallon, had escaped the complainant's notice: "We owe a huge gratitude to the men and women of our Armed Forces and salute their service in keeping us safe each and every day."

It is perfectly acceptable to eschew the outward forms represented by Armed Forces Day displays, just as it is to wear a white poppy or no poppy at all. Many of us are guided by our consciences to make these choices. And it is strangely – possibly wilfully – short-sighted to see this as disrespect for the men and women of the armed forces. The current manifestation of Armed Forces Day should not be be beyond critical questioning. The tabloids like to present dissent as 'snubs' to opinions which they have played a significant part in forming, but Quakers are not alone in being disturbed by the packaging of the gear and tackle of armed conflict as family entertainment. If you doubt that such packaging is a recruiting ploy, consider this from Colonel David Allfrey, former head of the Army's recruitment strategy: "Our new model is about raising awareness, and that takes a ten-year span. It starts with a seven-year-old boy seeing a parachutist at an air show and thinking 'that looks great'. From then on, the army is trying to build interest by drip, drip, drip". Colonel Allfrey, described the follow-up of the dripping in these words: "The army careers advisers who operate in schools are skilled salesmen".

So your seven-year-old may be very excited to get the opportunity of wearing an oversized helmet and sitting behind a machine gun on Armed Forces Day, but do not be deceived. This is not about respect for the skill and courage of military personnel. It is carefully contrived advertising aimed at the vulnerable.

The Quaker Meeting of which I am a member held a silent vigil in the Peace Garden of an East Anglian market town on Armed Forces Day this year. We have done this for several years and always advertise it in the same way – "we emphasise our belief that the best way of supporting the country's military personnel is to work and pray for peace, peace-building and conflict resolution."

There is another way and its voice is a quiet one. Here is the American theologian Stanley Hauerwas: "As long as it is assumed that war is always an available option, we will not be forced to imagine any alternative to war".

Let us be imaginative. Pageantry and conformity are neither indices of respect nor tools of peace.

Propaganda and quiet processes
June 27, 2015

Clichés are usually truths which have somewhat lost their impact through repetition. That repetition takes place because the truths concerned were originally mordantly appropriate. Try out 'If war is the answer, what is the question?' and ' if all you have is a hammer, everything looks like a nail'.

These are both salient truths when considering the creeping militarisation of society – particularly in our schools – and the part played in this by Armed Forces Day.

The displays which take place on this day, though ostensibly about showing support for members of the armed forces, have more to do with boosting recruitment and entrenching an uncritical and unquestioning attitude in the public mind. Indeed, try suggesting that displays of military hardware and pageantry which present armed conflict as family entertainment might leave something to be desired, and you are likely to be met with indignant opposition and a refusal to entertain the idea that there might be a darker underlay to all the excitement. Sentiment has been corrupted into a sentimentality which is marginalising questioning voices.

The spectacle of military ceremonial and the excitement of being offered the opportunity to sit in a helicopter gunship or handle an assault rifle deflects the attention away from the horrors of armed conflict and its life-deforming aftermath. Adolescent boys, who may be struggling with a model of masculinity very much predicated on power and strength, are particularly vulnerable to such seductive messages and presentations. And this is where we need to remind ourselves that the British Army – alone in the European Union – still recruits 16 year-olds into its ranks.

Around £45 million has been spent by the Department for Education in funding the 'military ethos' for schools over the last three years. The Ministry of Defence puts £180 million into running the Combined Cadet Force in schools and during the past year, the Department for Education has promoted the 'British Armed Forces Learning Resource' to every school. Educationalists have criticised this for what they describe as poor quality learning materials and biased, politically motivated content. School resources are also provided for Armed Forces Day and are described by Forces Watch as displaying "a wholly sanitised image of military activity".

Veterans for Peace, an educational organisation of former military personnel dedicated to increasing public awareness of the costs of war, says: "The army look to the youngest recruits (from age 16) to fill the most dangerous jobs in the armed forces because these jobs tend to be under-recruited. The Ministry of Defence says that enlisting from such a young age allows the army to make up for recruitment shortfalls, 'particularly for the infantry'". Veterans for Peace also point to a 2013 study carried out by ForcesWatch and Child Soldiers International, which looked at British army fatalities in Afghanistan and found that soldiers who enlisted aged 16 and completed their training were approximately twice as likely as adult recruits to die or be injured in conflict.

A video released by Veterans for Peace – *Action Man: Battlefield Casualties* – portrays a more realistic view of the outcomes of war and armed conflict on young bodies and minds. They describe it as being "intended to counter the recruitment propaganda of Armed Forces Day". Perhaps the voice of men and women who have been there, done that and bear the wounds, may have an impact beyond that of the 'usual suspects'.

A group of those suspects – Bury St Edmunds Quakers – gathered on the afternoon of Armed Forces Day in the garden of our Meeting

House in a silent vigil for peace. There were just 14 of us. It is easy to dismiss such actions as pointless – indeed, we may have our own occasional doubts when we see the power and influence arrayed against peace. But because we have other instruments in our world-view than the metaphorical hammer, we believe that we – and others who work for peace – have a vision wider than that 'nail' of projecting force as the solution to international problems. We believe that vision has the capacity to be transformative.

If an amount of money equal to the budget for influencing the young towards militarism was to be invested in peacemaking, conflict resolution, nation building and dialogue, 'unarmed forces' could become central to political, educational and diplomatic thinking.

By persisting in quiet questioning of the populist propaganda which the government is so eager to spread, while remaining steadfast in respect for men and women of the armed forces, we will gradually get across the message that support for their courage and sacrifice is not to be conflated with support for the futility which is war.

We must never lose faith in our "small circles and quiet processes."

Inversion: an Elegy for Ivor Gurney

Yearning from a foul slit in bludgeoned earth, the song-making soldier
dreamed of sun silvering Severn and of firstlight in the hair of girls;
saw tea laid in bloodied land; his mother's face along the wire.
Only these the pledges of sanity.

Men called him mad and took him far from home.
The music tells of heart in retreat:
harmony straining to the unattainable tonic falters,
crumbles to consummation of humanity.

Here was a mind whole; here soul surviving.
Reaching for what once had meaning
makes madness plain: reason
dwells with the ruined.

'We are many'
July 1, 2015

Yesterday, I wept in a cinema – something I had not done since, at the age of 10, I was utterly undone by the death of Bambi's mother. The cause of tears on this occasion was a scene from Amir Amirani's film 'We are Many', a documentary about the global protest against the Iraq War.

The scene concerned came at the film's emotional pivot point – the immense sense of hope generated by the astounding world-wide resistance to the 2003 invasion of Iraq giving way to the terrible images of high explosive ordinance tearing Baghdad apart. This was followed by all but unbearable footage of George Bush giving a post-conflict after-dinner speech. The President of the United States offered his audience "a slide show" in which people were shown peering under desks and riffling through drawers in the Oval Office, with inane commentary from the Commander in Chief of the 'victorious' forces about not being able to find any weapons of mass destruction. This was inter-cut with images of the war's aftermath: of shattered bodies lying in bombed streets, of traumatised, mute children and of aged faces, blank and distant with despair. It drove the vast, cynical and ruinous deceit of Bush and his eager sidekick Tony Blair into the heart with greater power than any number of words could hope to achieve.

But a pivot point only exists where there is momentum. The narrative went on to remind us that the protest of 15 February 2003 was not a dead end. Something had been sown in our collective awareness which was to bear fruit ten years later.

On 29 August 2013, David Cameron failed to win a Commons vote for British military action in Syria. The debate had acknowledged the power of public anti-war feeling which was the heritage of the Iraq disaster. Philip Hammond, then Defence Secretary, saw this through a different glass, claiming that the Iraq war had "poisoned the well" of public opinion, and would "place some strain" on US-UK relationships. Democracy can be uncomfortable that way.

President Obama – more of a democrat than Hammond – realised that the climate of public opinion meant that the issue of military action had to be taken to Congress. And there, it was defeated.

Despite the windy rhetoric of Bush: "this [9/11] isn't an act of terrorism: it's an act of war" and Blair: "we take your struggle as our struggle...let us reorder the world around us"; despite the apparent boast of Colin Powell's Chief of Staff, Colonel Lawrence Wilkerson that "we got people believing that Saddam Hussein was connected with 9/11" and despite the blatant misrepresentations made about Saddam's 'weapons of mass destruction', the lies did not take root in the minds of millions around the world. In 790 cities across 72 countries; in every continent – including Antarctica where staff at the US McMurdo research station were later fired for their participation – millions of people marched and demonstrated.

Power was shaken into a degree of self-examination and some of the shaking came from unexpected sources. "It shut you up", observed Lord Falconer, one of Tony Blair's closest allies in 2003, who now believes that the Iraq war was "a mistake". Lawrence Wilkerson, now regretting his role, says the US government "perpetuated a hoax." Hans Blix, the UN weapons inspector said in the aftermath of Blair's 2002 Commons statement on Saddam's 'weapons of mass destruction': "Tony Blair lost his credibility in those 45 minutes".

The biggest day of international protest the world has ever seen did not succeed in holding back politicians bent on war. Questions were raised about the relationship between government and democracy which have not been answered and which will remain. But the enormity of what was done and the scale of the international response of 'not in my name' have left a deep imprint on the consciousness of both governors and governed. Tony Benn, speaking at a rally in the days leading up to war, urged: "Anger at injustice, optimism for a better world." The anti-war movement has given the 'many' a focus for that anger and optimism. It has set a marker which will not be erased.

Shelley's Mask of Anarchy, written as a statement of non-violent resistance in the aftermath of the Peterloo Massacre, and from which the film takes its title, confirms both that power of the human spirit and our call to believe in and nourish it:

> Rise, like lions after slumber
> In unvanquishable number!
> Shake your chains to earth like dew
> Which in sleep had fallen on you:
> Ye are many – they are few!

Peace in Europe: a precious legacy demeaned
May 12, 2016

David Cameron has suggested that Brexit could put European peace at risk. Never knowingly undersold in absurdity, Boris Johnson, before mumble-singing the first three words of Beethoven's setting of *Ode to Joy*, ridiculed him with a reference to Germany crossing the border into France.

This kind of political vaudeville demeans the very concept of peace making and keeping, of conflict avoidance and resolution, of memory, sorrow and of the responsibility which we all bear for making it possible for populations to live and flourish in freedom from war. It is historically and morally illiterate and is contrived to sow fear.

I am old enough (as is Johnson) to have experienced the shadow of the war which ended in the decade before I was born. As a young child, I saw around me men – still in youth or early middle-life – whose bodies had been fractured by war. I had too, a child's incomplete awareness of the ruin wrought in minds and souls by physical horror and tormented consciences.

The founding fathers of what was to become the European Union belonged to that wounded generation and to the one which was formed by the war of 1914-18. Churchill, Schuman, De Gaulle, Adenauer, Heath and their younger contemporaries, were formed by the two huge conflicts of the 20th century which had their origins, if not their ultimate boundaries, in Europe. For these men, 'never again' had a meaning which we must neither lose nor cheapen in pursuit of lesser goals.

As the last generation to have experienced the horror of continental war passes, so too may our understanding of the irenic agency of sharing economic power and a degree of sovereignty. Ties of shared interest, cooperation and knowledge are the enemies of that concept of 'otherness' which may be exploited for alienation and hostility in times of difference. It is in the spreading of that shared interest that we may best maintain what was envisaged in the Schuman Declaration of May 1950.

That vision realised that coal and steel – the raw materials of weapons production – were key to ensuring that nation states which had long seen their military-industrial complexes as the tools of competing empires, would instead develop a common interest. Battleships and bombers were to be beaten into BMWs and railways. Thus the European Coal and Steel Community, the forerunner of the EU, gave us the connection to sustainable peace in words which are still relevant almost seven decades later: "The pooling of coal and steel production... will change the destinies of those regions which have long been devoted to the manufacture of munitions of war, of which they have been the most constant victims."

Of course Europe has, during those decades, been subject to incidences of failure which mark the human condition. There has been armed conflict in the former Yugoslavia, Ukraine and Crimea. But these are not EU states and though a Europe committed to peace must consider its responsibilities and its potential here, let us not lose sight of the fact that it is truly impossible to imagine France and Germany ever at war again.

It is this seed of cooperation sown in the psyche of Europe which has inspired and kept peace. Steel and coal were the engines of moral movement among millions of Europeans. That role was not, and never will be, fulfilled by NATO. A military alliance, requiring its members to contribute two per cent of their GDP for armaments, is as for removed from that redemptive vision of changing the destinies of nations, once bounded by the making and usage of weaponry, as it is possible to conceive. It can never be an instrument of peace.

Peace is not just the absence of war. It is the choice to strive for understanding and solidarity, to root out injustice and hatred in ourselves and others, to make policies which will enable the sowing of peace and to cultivate societies which will sustain it. This is our legacy from statesmen who had seen their continent sundered and deformed by total war twice in the space of 25 years.

And it is far too precious an inheritance to be demeaned by the ahistoric and morally inadequate knockabout of shallow, opportunistic politicians.

This will not be our finest hour
December 7, 2015

We have to hope that committing a country's armed forces to acts of war is one of the hardest decisions a politician ever has to make and one which makes the greatest demand on conscience. But observation makes hard to rid oneself of a suspicion that many senior politicians have a not-so-secret desire to play the role of war leader.

Remember Margaret Thatcher in headscarf and goggles posing in the turret of a tank during the Falklands war? Tony Blair striving to appear blokish and casual in shirt-sleeves against a backdrop of bored-looking soldiers in Iraq? George Bush on the flight-deck of an aircraft carrier, sporting a USAF bomber jacket? And on Saturday, we saw the Defence Secretary, Michael Fallon at RAF Akrotiri with a fighter plane in soft-focus behind him, unable to suppress a smirk as he proclaimed: "We will hit them harder".

"Every man thinks meanly of himself for not having been a soldier", said Samuel Johnson. There does seem to be something in the male psyche – though it does not belong exclusively to that gender – which finds vicarious glory and a sense of power in all the tackle of armed conflict. Maybe this has its roots in our primate natures – watch the larger, more powerful animal use its stature and weight to frighten or dominate a smaller creature. In the boardroom, the pub, the street or the international arena, there is still something of the jungle in us.

What is basic may quickly become base when it is not kept in check by analysis and moral reflection. Where these civilising attributes are absent, the prioritisation of force over other responses is inevitable. The thin case made by David Cameron for UK air strikes has made this disturbingly clear.

Rhetoric is the principal instrument of politicians' love affair with military force and of all the speeches which have followed the terrible events in Paris, Hilary Benn's seemed to me the most dangerous. It combined skilful deployment of the techniques of rhetorical discourse with a poor grasp of the immense complexities of the Syrian conflict. Behind its actorly cadences – as with so much grandiose peroration on the exercise of armed force – was a ghostly echo of Churchill's oratory from a different war, a different time and a very different geo-politics.

It is significant that memories of our 'finest hour' still inform – even though on a subliminal level – so much about our present-day responses when the war-shout goes up. The generation which lived and suffered through World War 2 has almost passed and when living memory dwindles, legend-making and a tendency to romantic illusions gain ground.

"All war is a symptom of man's failure as a thinking animal." These are the words of John Steinbeck and politicians are unlikely to want us to reflect upon them. Not least, because they remind us that however evil we may perceive our antagonist to be, we must bear at least some responsibility for his flourishing.

It would be idle to expect many politicians to share the Quaker view that true peace cannot be imposed by military might and that ideas can never be eradicated by bombs. But it is not unreasonable to question the eagerness of our elected leaders to deck themselves in the garb of warrior chiefs. The decision to go to war should always be a last resort, better clothed in sackcloth and ashes and expressed in the plain speech of sorrow for our collective failure.

Seasons of Life

Ageing Writer

Years are slithery things.
There seem to be plenty then you find you have
dropped some.
Greying hair, spectacles, a couple of teeth lost,
memories of worse and better times.
Once there was a man in this house.
Now there isn't. But it's alright
because on the other side of pain
there is understanding.
Friends come and mostly stay.
Ideas excite, words invite grasp,
caress and struggle.
There may still be love because there
always has been.

It will be there at the end.

Convalescence and a small transfiguration
June 6, 2016

Last weekend, strolling round a nature reserve, I saw something so beautiful it took my breath for a moment – a rabbit, nibbling on summer-lit grass with the summer sun shining through the membranes of its ears: a commonplace creature momentarily transfigured.

The circumstances of this little epiphany were significant. Ten weeks earlier I had undergone surgery for a detached retina and this was my first solo outing behind the new spectacles which had put me at liberty to drive once more and – in combination with the skill of a surgical team – given me back the use of my right eye and made the left one serviceable again.

I have no intention of dwelling on surgical detail but what I learned during those weeks of initial forced inactivity, followed by ongoing dependency and vulnerability have an application far beyond my personal and temporary inconvenience.

I have been young and am not yet so old. I have been blessed with a robust constitution and beyond a few broken bones and an adult attack of chickenpox, I have had little acquaintance with physical impairment. This was the first time the fabric really had failed and it came as a shock.

When one is used to autonomy and, within the bounds of ability and morality, unimpeded agency, accepting restriction is difficult, but it also offers a gateway into heightened perception and the grace of accepting need met by kindness. And when the normal props are, even temporarily, stripped away, you have to sort theory from true conviction.

During the 72 post-operative hours in which I had to lie still in one position, I own myself sorely tested in this regard. Unable to read, in some discomfort and with no certainty that the operation would prove successful, I was a spectacular spiritual failure. I tried daily to hold a one-woman Meeting for Worship and I would not have been surprised if the Spirit had moved on in search of a more receptive heart. "And yet, and yet..." It is in the space made by that ellipsis that I have come to find meaning in this disagreeable experience.

"Someone will put a belt around you and lead you where you would not go." We probably prefer not to dwell too long on Jesus' words to Peter. Most of us will of course, not be called to martyrdom as presaged by this warning. But that powerlessness is the daily, monthly, yearly, even life-long experience of many people. Disability, chronic sickness,

77

poverty, exclusion and the fear associated with these conditions make for lives which differ hugely from the experience of those of us who are more fortunate. Without compassionate help, respect, friendship and love, minds and souls splinter into despair. My fleeting visit to the outermost edge of this terrain has shown me how much more we need each other than we may imagine; how necessary it is for us all to keep our wits alive to the realities of need; how responsible every single one of us, whatever our calling, is for our neighbour. Politicians, please reflect.

If I had the skills of an artist, I would paint that glow-eared rabbit as an icon to focus my chastened spirit on the gentle instruction of the Spirit.

How doubt redeems belief
July 8, 2009

Music is served by silence. Mass requires space, both around and within: consider the grace and eloquence of a sculpture by Barbara Hepworth or Henry Moore. That which is unrelieved, without antithesis or contrast, fails to convince and tends to sclerosis. As with art, so with faith. Where there is no doubt – or no admission of doubt – faith has no 'other' to give it shape and reference, no perspective enabling the vision of a larger landscape.

On 3 July, many Christian traditions celebrate the feast of the apostle who has become known as Doubting Thomas. I will own to a devotion to this very human and confused follower of Jesus. For me, faith has always been difficult but it is also something without which I feel incomplete and which never quite goes away: a dominant pedal gathering me up and directing me towards some as yet unheard harmonic resolution.

Once past the unquestioning belief of early childhood, I was held in my wavering course by the understated and slightly unorthodox faith of my parents. They never required me to believe six impossible things before breakfast, never offered theological definitions and never tried to win the arguments which arose from my teenage stroppiness. Being secure in their own faith and having experienced the ebb and flow of belief in living through the hardships and losses of war, they simply let their lives speak.

There have been three distinct, faith-nourishing experiences in my life. The first dates from my early teens and gives me an insight into the meaning of 'becoming as little children'. My father was dis-assembling his motorbike – a task which always seemed to consume far more time than actually riding it – and as I passed him spanners and oily rags, I was protesting at the incomprehensibility of God. My immature and wholly solipsistic argument ran something like this: "if there is a God, why can't he fix it so that we know? Why do people always say it's a mystery? How do we know it's true if we don't understand it?"

Dad sighed gently as he always did when I was being difficult and pointed to our dog who was idly scratching himself amongst the scattered vitals of the BSA: "Look at Django. He's got no idea of how to put this engine back together. Doesn't mean it can't be done." That was all. And the impact it still has on me decades later suggests that it was sufficient.

Not long after this exchange, my father died suddenly and my creaky adolescent faith was tipped over into an angry and desolate atheism. Philip Larkin's disturbing lines on religion laid me low then and still have the power to do so: "that vast moth-eaten musical brocade, created to pretend we never die". The words precisely catch and cruelly define that fear that our credos may all be the result of existential terror and denial. The dead are gone as we will one day be gone. Their absence tears at our existence and we long beyond measure to see them again whilst dreading that we never will. That was the condition of Thomas whose grief and shock at the execution of his beloved rabbi was such that the excited protestations of his friends must have seemed like delusion and madness.

During my period of atheism, there was another memorable occasion when simple words took root and have remained a source of light. A fellow undergraduate, who is now a priest, gently and without dogma or dialectic, spoke to my confusion. Pouring me a Guinness, he observed "well, I just think that faith does better things than doubt."

The third occasion was of an entirely different magnitude. It happened ten years ago in an intensive care unit as my mother's life came to its end. In those last few terrible minutes, we felt an immense presence 'come for her'. I have longed to recapture that astounding experience, to draw upon it for comfort and validation. But the transcendent is not so biddable and the tensions between faith and doubt remain when we temporal, finite creatures clutch at the eternal and infinite.

None of these faith-sustaining experiences owe anything to orthodox teaching, biblical exegesis or force of theological argument. What they have in common, in varying degrees, is the experience of love – its actions and consequences. That was what happened to Thomas. No rabbinical exposition, no references to Torah. Just "put your hand here in my side." Whether or not the account is literal or allegorical (the agnostic in me speaks), it is true on the level which speaks to the heart. And despite the value of the intellectual aspects of belief, it is the experiential which, in the end, keeps us going.

In childhood, I began to learn of humility before the unknowable; in youth, to start to believe that positive choices are in themselves an act of faith; in maturity, to catch a glimpse of that power of love which survives our bodily dissolution. To fear one's doubts and to deny them, is to take away the silence from the music and the space from the sculpture. As with all untruth, denial demeans, diminishes and eventually destroys. It is in acknowledging doubt that faith is brought into focus. And it is only now, in my sixth decade, that I have learned to doubt my doubts and to be less fearful of uncertainty. I believe, help thou my unbelief.

April 2014

April snow sparks in high gullies of
cloud-patched land.
Below, first green mists the hedgebones
along the wath where we
gather in walking remembrance.

Spaced with our steps, words fall slow.
Memory and ambiguity measure out the silences
of our learning.
What we had always known comes
fledgling tender;
a new understanding, ancient as the fell-flanks.

Easter silence
April 22 2014

The long religious and secular weekend is over. The Bank Holiday draws to an end and the liturgical celebrations of Easter have reached their climax. As Quakers do not keep these 'times and seasons', I find myself caught in a challenging no-woman's land at Easter and Christmas.

Over the last few days, my Twitter timeline has been full of reflection, exaltation and alleluias. Clergy have shared their anxieties over Easter candles, choirs, sermons and fatigue. They have celebrated the completion of their celebrations with bacon butties, gin, chocolate and a general sense of tension unbuttoned and well-earned relaxation.

In the betwixt and between land of the Peculiar People, Easter is acknowledged. But there are no forms nor dressed altars. The Meeting House looks just the same on Easter Sunday as it does on all the other First Days of the year. Sometimes vocal ministry will make reference to the season. Often, it will not.

This Sunday, I was more grateful than ever for the deep and gathered silence. I have no belief in the physical resurrection, holding instead to a sense of wondering gratitude that Jesus – the man whom an elderly Friend of my Meeting once so memorably described as "a man with a genius for God" – endures in the hearts, minds and lives of so many of us. But the mystery of death will not, for me, be so easily rolled away.

It seems particularly poignant to reflect on that mystery this year. My nonagenarian auntie entered into her peace just a month ago. The last few months have been filled with anxiety, sadness and fatigue as we made our various ways up and down to northern Cumbria. To sit beside the increasing frailness of her body and, in the last weeks, the clouding of her mind, has been painful. The cessation of physical existence is indeed an immense mystery and I know of no evidence that any have returned from beyond its horizon. Nonetheless, I do not doubt for a moment that she has returned to her Source.

But because silence offers the space to bring these thoughts, because it does not belabour me with victorious hymns or dragoon me into shouts of rejoicing, I may yet find my way there. Perhaps it is a form of via negativa – in exploring what is not and what I am unable to accept, I may eventually learn 'what is'.

For me, right now, only silence respects that cloud of unknowing.

Lifting up our eyes to the hills
May 16, 2012

This is a small and densely populated island. Most of us live in urban or semi-urban environments. Even if we are fortunate enough to have some space around us, it is likely that work will take us into the area of traffic jams, parking problems, overcrowded trains, queues and their attendant frustrations.

I have just returned from a few days in my native place. Most of Cumbria has a population density of less than 100 people per square kilometre. In London, the average is 11,500. If you proceed vertically rather than horizontally, the Cumbrian ratio becomes even smaller. And when I ascended Coniston Old Man last week, the number of people I encountered during six hours on the fell barely got into double figures.

The sense of proportion – in more than just the literal sense – which is gained by being on high land and in open space is remarkable. To stand 2600 feet up and see the landscape unfurl beneath you is breathtaking. Coniston Water glittered like a tiny ribbon of glass far below and the hazy outline of the Isle of Man could just be made out on the horizon. Although I was looking at no more than one part of one area of a small country, the scale of the panorama was a reminder of the relation of the human person to the landmass on which we live out our often heedless existence. It is hard to remain preoccupied with the micro when the macro is present with such intensity.

The need for space does not end with the physical. The metaphysical awareness which enables us to make our common lives just and fruitful is more likely to thrive when we are not pressed upon by our environment. The sense of ease and the intimations of creative humility which are conferred by a large landscape points up the necessity of 'making space' in our collective and personal interactions. In politics, the media, faith bodies, education, commerce, industry – in fact, in all situations where decisions have to be taken, the capacity to 'stand back' from self should be nurtured.

Instinctive opposition and the ego-based partisanship which must win an argument rather than find a way forward through dialogue, has become the norm. It is worth taking longer to arrive and to travel better. That may mean accepting that there does not always have to be an answer or that a neat conclusion must be reached in a prescribed time frame. It requires us to venture into an intellectual, emotional and spiritual space where acknowledging one's smallness in the greater landscape becomes possible.

The type of interactions seen in parliaments, synods, boardrooms and many current affairs programmes form much of our thinking on decision making. They are the dialectical equivalent of the busy street and the overcrowded train. Taking time to lift up our eyes – and if possible, our boots – to the hills restores a closeness with the real nature of our being and offers a better view.

House Clearance

Ninety years of life gathers.
It fills cupboards and drawers;
throngs attic and shed.
Our tasks bring a communion:
– Oh, look! – Do you remember..?
And taking from her store things both old and new,
we find the commonwealth of heaven is very near.

Simplicity is about appropriate living
November 11, 2009

Simplicity can be complex. It is perhaps the most attractive of the Quaker Testimonies but also the most difficult to grasp and give expression to in daily life. It may easily be confused with austerity and it certainly offers plentiful openings into dead ends to those of us who have a leaning towards Puritanism.

Early Friends referred to this Testimony as 'plainness' and bore witness to it in their forms of dress and speech. George Fox warned his followers to "keep your testimony against the world's vain fashions" and to this day, there is still a tendency amongst Quakers to dress in a modest and unobtrusive manner.

English speech of the seventeenth century still made use of the formal 'you' and the familiar 'thou'. Quakers would choose the familiar form, regardless of the status of an interlocutor, in order to bear witness to their belief in equality. The custom still persists in our occasional usage today, particularly in the north of England where one may still hear older Friends say "thank God for thy ministry" or speak of "holding thee in the light".

These choices, made in order to avoid whatever might contribute to social division, may therefore be perceived as closely allied to the Testimonies of peace and equality.

As with all disciplines, 'plainness' may become an end in itself rather than a means of growing closer to the truth. Margaret Fell, sometimes known as the 'nursing mother' of Quakerism, warned, in characteristically robust and memorable fashion, against a contemporary obsession with outward appearance to the detriment of attending to the leadings of the spirit: "but we must all be in one dress and one colour: this is a silly poor gospel".

Fell urged Friends to seek rather to be "covered with God's eternal spirit and clothed with his eternal light." The warning has not been outworn. Three centuries later, the temptation to mistake means for ends is still with us

A more constructive view of what constitutes simplicity, and one which I strive to take as my guide, was offered by an 18th century Quaker, John Woolman, who preached against 'cumber' – the habit of cluttering one's physical and spiritual environment with unnecessary possessions and desires which complicate our lives and divert us from perception and acting out of the truth. This involves positive choices rather than negative austerity, although it is easy to mistake the latter for evidence of simplicity.

A family possessed of sufficient disposable income to replace their kitchen may opt for the fashionable simplicity of the Shaker style. If the original kitchen was still serviceable, though less 'plain', then this is surely nothing more than an expensive following of "vain fashion". Satiety mimicking the appearance of simplicity is a particularly distressing form of delusion. For if simplicity is not seen as the servant of truth, then truth is obscured. If truth is obscured, simplicity will have no integrity. This circle of meaning is summed up in the words of Rufus Jones, an American academic and writer who was also a Quaker: "unclouded honesty at the heart and centre of a man is the true basis of simplicity".

However, simplicity requires more of us than the shunning of fashion trends. At its heart is not just the nature of our material goods, but also our attitude towards those goods. In an acquisitive, consumerist culture which makes quick and shallow assessments of an individual's worth based upon their lifestyle, a refusal to acquire without the exercise of discernment or self-discipline is essential for those who would be a sign of contradiction.

If we decline to differentiate between wants and needs, we not only contribute to injustice and environmental degradation, we manifest that the source of our dignity and self-esteem lies in our purchasing power rather than in our common dignity as children of one Creator.

Simplicity in our own day is inseparable from peace and sustainability. The simple life, freely chosen, is described in Quaker thinking as "a source of strength". It has the capacity to inoculate us against the greed which lies at the root of conflict.

John Woolman was aware of the danger: "May we look upon our treasures, and the furniture of our houses, and the garments in which we array ourselves, and try whether the seeds of war have any nourishment in these our possessions or not."

Simplicity presents a radical challenge to a world order predicated on ever growing riches and ease. It is an order which tends to the growth of inequality and injustice. It seeks short-term gain for the developed world at the expense of the poorest, of the capacity of our planet to endure the diminution of its resources and the increase of waste and pollution which we pour upon it in the unconsidered gratification of our acquisitive egos.

Simplicity is perhaps best understood as appropriate living. It is about owning and using only what is necessary and not being seduced by that which is dangled before us by advertisers and arbiters of style. It is about focusing less on our own desires and more upon the common good. It is about vigilance over uncritical susceptibility to cultural norms. It is about having a clear vision of our origin and our end. Above all, it is about understanding what is needed if we are to love our neighbours as ourselves.

Retired Fell Farmer

He came down off the tops last back end.
After sixty years on steep acres,
his kingdom ceded to a son
who has no time to visit.
Now he rolls through the greystone town
on warped legs. Fast to his heels,
the border collie sets at prams,
flat-eared with anxiety, not daring to dart
on level land.
An old man and an old dog
in a futile season.

A fanfare for the uncommon (wo)man
March 16, 2018

The man on the Clapham omnibus, the man on the street, Joe Public. There have been many labels over the years for what are generally considered to be 'ordinary people'.

The categories of politicians and pollsters are a little more blatant in their condescension: Mondeo Man, Worcester Woman, Pebble-dash People. These are calculated to create distance and at the same time to create a bogus aura of respect and understanding. It is no coincidence that Jesus' words 'salt to the world', conferring noble purpose and high calling, are so often degraded to 'salt of the earth', a patronising reach-me-down on the tongues of the middle class when praising their gardeners, nannies and cleaners.

'Ordinary' is an angle of gaze. It is sometimes enlarging to tilt the head or change the focal length. Art – in that breath-catching capacity to make the everyday sacred and salvific – is so often to be found in humble frames and unremarkable dwellings.

The East London Group of painters were active during the years 1928 to 1936. The best known among them are probably Harold and Walter Steggles, working class London boys whose passion for art was nourished through John Cooper's art classes at the Bromley and Bow Institute. The social landscape of the artists of this group was that of clerks, factory workers and craftspeople. Some, like Brynhild Parker, were the children of a slightly higher social stratum, though none of them were what would now be considered movers and shakers. But they were rooted people who all embraced and honoured the extraordinary qualities of the ordinary.

The East London artists painted unfashionable streets, humble, sometimes shabby, interiors and rural landscapes, particularly in East Anglia. In doing so, they both recorded much which is now changed beyond recognition and offered those glimpses of transformation which may change and sustain lives. To me, there is a sacramental quality in Brynhild Parker's depiction of a breakfast table by the window of a first floor room painted in 1930: a chimney stack and a plain house front provide the view, while a milk bottle, bowl and a plate bearing a heel of bread are transformed into utensils of grace by the artist's treatment of light. Many of us will have seen something similar a thousand times, but here we are arrested and offered the immense gift of looking again at the quotidian. Here is the mountain top offered in the lodging-house room, here a reminder of the altar of the carpenter's bench and of the eternal value of sparrows.

This visionary potential of the everyday is not confined to the visual arts. I find another outlier of eternity in the poems of John Clare. The 'peasant poet' who lived such an obscure and ultimately painful life, observed the natural world as only one who lived, breathed and walked among the small and overlooked sphere of fur, feather, plough, lane and copse could do. The farm labourer's son who died in the Northampton Lunatic Asylum in 1864, was undone by the dispossession of enclosure. That bone-of-bone connection with place has been largely diminished to a USP in our own time. As the standing from which the inbreathing of meaning and clear-sighted experience makes possible an exhalation of universal authenticity, truth and power, it is all but done with. Such is the alienating force of ambition and deracination.

In 1942, Aaron Copland composed 'Fanfare for the Common Man' in response to a speech given by Henry Wallace in which the US Vice-President proclaimed the 'dawning of the century of the common man'. It is an engaging enough piece of music. But it seems to me to miss the essence of remaining close to rooted experience under the gracious illumination of humility. Despite the hauteur of the sophisticated and successful, something good came out of Nazareth.

Seasons of Death

Farmer's Funeral

We saw his tractor as we came from the church.
Left untouched in the days since darkness
had fallen fast on full day, it remained
cross-furrow on the new-turned earth;
high rigged and outridden by broad wheels,
a small craft
standing off from the mother-ship
across a sea of graves.

Winding the south wall, we followed his coffin –
as flocks of birds will the fore-striking plough –
to the acre's edge where that rich earth
had been opened for him.
And beyond the wykegate,
his grandchildren, released from solemnity,
ran down the lane to the welcome
of the enduring house.

A death in the square and the light that will never go out
November 29, 2017

There are times when the need to report and comment on large scale events can seem overwhelming. The general narrative of cruelty, violence, self-seeking and mendacity presses on the mind and spirit and in distorting the vision, makes us feel powerless.

So here, now, I want to step back a little to reflect on a life which is the antithesis of all that bears down upon us daily.

Two days ago, a neighbour a few doors around the square died. Ken (not his real name), was a skilled tradesman who had worked in the building industry for most of his life. He contracted mesothelioma from exposure to asbestos and his death, though slow in coming, was inevitable.

We live on a small estate which is like many others around the country. It is part of that social stratum in which, for all it flaws, I feel generally comfortable – where the skilled working class meets and mingles with the lower middle class. There are occasional outbursts of middle-England indignation and Residents' Association pettiness, but on the whole, the people here are sensible and friendly.

Ken was both sensible and friendly. But he was more. He was that precious thing, a good neighbour. He would be out clearing snow in the winter, always with a particular care for the elderly or disabled. He cut his next-door neighbour's hedge without any fuss or angling for thanks: "well, I've got the trimmer out..." Every summer he mowed the grass of another neighbour who had a bad back and he was always ready to fix small domestic malfunctions.

His was an unpolished but genuine kindness. When the man with whom I shared my life for 20 years and I decided to go our separate ways, Ken touched my arm and said simply "Oh mate, I'm sorry". That meant more than many protestations that were offered with greater eloquence..

Ken made no great noise in the world. His life revolved round his garden and the local dog track. He looked after racing greyhounds for other owners and they could not have been in better or more responsible hands. He was a loving father and although he and his wife never made any pretence that their marriage was always happy, they stayed together and raised their two children to be good people. Some would have ignored or patronised him, They could not have been more out of tune.

Ken's death was as unassuming and honest as his life. He decided against treatment, knowing that it could not stem the relentless course of his disease. The last time I talked with him, his words, spoken without bitterness or fear, were characteristic: "I've lasted longer than they thought I would. I just hope it's quick when it comes."

It was not. His last days were difficult despite the loving care of the hospice. He told his wife he was "ready to go", and his going was a mercy. I never heard him speak of spiritual matters nor to express any sense that he might survive bodily death.

There are countless men and women like Ken. Everything about them is unspectacular to eyes and ears attuned to a status conscious culture. Their qualities are not those which can be measured by the accepted metrics of influence. Their innate goodness and kindness is a very local phenomenon but it is what makes our lives worthwhile. They are greater than all the world's tyrants, bullies, haters and self-publicists and their light will never go out.

Mourner's Kaddish

A winter afternoon: late light filling the windows with sky
chances sudden reflection.
The pithead gear, angled insect-frail against framed cloud and
chimney rim, startles my childheart, turns earth that meaning
may root.

In last years, mind moves to the most dear.
Wastwater was my mother's wish and standing beside her that early
spring morning,
I wondered again at the eye taken unawares.
Whin Rigg, twice-made in glass-still water:
perfect inversion of
earthmass.

This memory: her gentle touch on my shoulder,
acknowledging meaning in the silence;
verifying changelessness, honouring the new strangeness.
Magnified and sanctified…
In her days and in my lifetime,
Magnified and sanctified.

A ceremonial funeral and a common destiny
April 18, 2013

"Lying here, she is one of us, subject to the common destiny of all human beings". Speaking at Margaret Thatcher's funeral, the Bishop of London reminded us of what a funeral is actually about.

Whether this ceremonial event could really bring us to the recognition of our commonality and of the consequent need for humility, solidarity and compassion is open to question. This was a piece of political theatre, devised for an international audience and as such, it was carried out with that attention to detail and sense of pageantry which seems – to an Englishwoman – to be a particular skill of our national culture.

The tolling bells and muffled drums, the scarlet and gold of ceremonial military dress, the reversed rifles and all the tackle and trim of warriors have a profound effect upon the observer. They are designed to stir something within us which bypasses discernment and strikes deep to unexamined and visceral response. In that sense, it is worth considering that they may have something in common with pornography. None of us are so pure that we may float serenely above these diversions from integrity.

The manner of our lives will be reflected in the observance of our passing. Allowing for the differences in station, our funerals will speak of what we really are. There were some aspects of Margaret Thatcher's funeral which were admirable and reflected her Methodist upbringing – her desire that there should be no eulogies and the consequent willingness to put herself in the hands of those who will speak of truths transcending the currency of political spin, was a flash of honesty among the dramaturgy of power and establishment. Richard Chartres – an establishment prelate to his backbone – rose to that challenge and spoke with greater insight, compassion and honesty than I had expected.

Nonetheless, the extravagance – in both the literal and ceremonial sense, revealed a deficit in truth. Comparisons may be odious, but it is sometimes useful to examine relational experience. My mother was of Margaret Thatcher's generation and was, like her, the daughter of a provincial working class family. A child of the west Cumbrian coalfield, she had a hard childhood and was left a young widow. She lived a life of simplicity, love and quiet dignity. These were therefore the qualities which informed her funeral. Anything else would have stolen her from us in a way that death could not.

The integrity which existed between her life and our farewell to her existence in this circle of being was, of course, not put under strain by the expectations of a wider audience. But it was the essential nature of that life and not its outward forms which made the last observances what they were.

If we have really understood and internalised that common destiny of which the bishop spoke, we must not only live so as to be ready for death, we will need to make our relationships, work and actions consonant with a truthful funeral. And in the face of that common destiny, the truth is in humility, in solidarity with our shared condition and in the constant vigilance of serving without hubris.

Deep looking and deep listening in the service of change
August 30, 2016

A series of 82 portraits by David Hockney portrays his sitters – famous and unknown, adults and children – in an identical format: every subject using the same chair and inhabiting the same space.

These works are striking because they are the result of a particular way of seeing. What could have been mechanical and unremarkable is transformed by the heightened gaze. Just as memorable poetry is created from intensified language and great music from mining the deepest lodes of sound, this kind of creativity is the fruit of spaciousness, of time taken and of the quick response interrogated.

The way in which we think and form our responses to the issues and questions which shape our common life frequently falls very short of this authentic approach. It is not difficult to see why. The media, in all its forms, not only requires, but demands an almost instantaneous response. Try pausing for thought in a radio interview and see panic enter your interlocutor's eyes. Watch and squirm as a politician attempts to give a nuanced answer to an absurdly weighted question and the interviewer goes for the jugular within five seconds. To hesitate is to have 'failed' the challenge. We should not be surprised that evasion and bluster is the learned response

Then there is the 'hit-back' reflex. Nowhere is this more apparent than in the bear-pit of social media. Not only is the ability to differ with respect and reason in short supply, there appear to be an alarming number of people who spend a good part of their day sitting on Twitter with no other purpose than the instant attack upon, or undermining of, any opinion which does not fit with their own. At a time when there is so much division over the Labour leadership and the conduct of the leadership election, this knee-jerkery is dispiriting. What could be a forum for thoughtful debate founded in listening becomes instead a series of loud-hailer assaults and rebuttals.

"Consider it possible you may be mistaken". This can be very difficult, but without it, there is no growth nor any space for learning, change, or indeed, for building conviction upon foundations of integrity. To look around an issue without sliding into comfortable short cuts provided by confirmation bias or habit takes time. Wherever possible, that time must be respected and where it is not available, we need to take up the challenge presented by remaining silent or admitting to being unsure. The three responses to questioning which were Clement Attlee's usual practice: 'Yes'. 'No' and 'I don't know' may no longer be possible, but the last option does have something to offer a culture at once insecure and combative.

Not to know, or to need more time to reflect, are not signs of weakness. Fast opinions may be as empty of nourishment as fast food and just as deleterious to well-being. The political, social, ethical and spiritual questions presented by a changing and interconnected world which is so often in conflict on both the macro and micro scales, asks of us something in which we are increasingly unpractised. If we would play a part in questioning and forming the fundamental values which shape our societies, we must go far beyond sharp and face-saving smartness. There is much we could learn from considering the focused respect of the creative artist's pursuit of meaning and from seeking sufficient courage to be humble.

Deep looking and deep listening – these are the habits which could transform our discourse and make it possible for people to talk and think about change in a way which cares more for truth and justice than for short-term domination.

Remembering Sarah
(23.1.95 – 14.6.95)

As a dragonfly will hang on air,
sprinkling summerlight before
baffling eyes in the quickness of its going,
you crossed our sight:
clear and prism-pure,
refracting immortality.

The voices that will not be drowned
August 29, 2010

"I hear those voices that will not be drowned". These words from Peter Grimes are pierced through the four-metre-high sculpture by Maggi Hambling which stands on the beach at Aldeburgh in celebration of the life and work of Benjamin Britten. Read against the Suffolk sky, they go straight to the heart.

For those of us whose working lives are passed in the gathering of, and comment upon, news, the space to stand away from the conveyor belt of the 'now' in order to reflect upon its enduring meaning, is sometimes difficult and always essential. The 48 hours we have just spent on the Suffolk coast and its hinterland has been a time of relaxation as expected, but also of unexpected and unlooked for revelation.

Hambling's sculpture of a vast scallop shell is astonishing. It is hard to believe that metal could be so fluid. From one angle, the fixed shape of the shell dominates. Viewed from another, it becomes all movement – waves undulating and breaking, seaweed flowing around rock. And always the words, inseparable from the scene, but apposite to all places and all times.

Ever since I first fell under the spell of Britten's music as an O-level pupil studying the St Nicholas Cantata, this coast has been part of the world of my imagination. Now, living much closer than I did all those years ago, I visit it whenever I can. The shingle beach does not draw bucket and spade holiday makers and the unmistakeable colouring of this eastern sea is not attractive to the compilers of holiday brochures. Whatever the hue of the immense East Anglian sky, the waters here remain a steely blue-grey with a brown undertone which reminds the onlooker of the earth against which the waves rush and withdraw.

I cannot look on this scene without hearing the high violins which open the first of the Sea Interludes from Peter Grimes. Never have a place and an artist been so closely knit together and it is hard to imagine a piece of art which could have better captured this emotional union than Hambling's scallop shell. The skill and vision of two great artists combined to speak of the divine spirit in a manner which took me entirely by surprise on this Bank Holiday excursion. Truly this was "a wind blowing from another country".

The church at Iken, just inland from Aldeburgh and a curlew's flight along the river Alde, stands on the site where St Botolph built a minster in the mid 7th century. The original foundation was destroyed by Vikings 200 years later and a new church built around 1070. Following the winding and narrow roads to this isolated church which stands in estuarine marshland , is to slip away a little from the 21st century and its preoccupations.

Driving between fields of sweet corn and sunflowers along lanes edged with drifts of sand, we were not surprised to be met by a sign welcoming us as pilgrims. And although our packs were in the boot of a car and a sat-nav had been our guide, we had – albeit unintentionally – come in the spirit of pilgrimage.

The small, partly thatched church has a simplicity and sanctity which causes a catch in the breath. The Norman nave, without decoration and rough rendered in stone and flint, is both ancient and timeless and if one stands facing west so as not to see the Victorian chancel, is undoubtedly a 'thin place' – a term in Celtic spirituality describing a location where the partition between our material world and the spiritual realm is insubstantial. Within these walls, forty generations have come to rejoice and to grieve; to bring their quotidian anxieties and their life-changing decisions. It is a place where "prayer has been made valid".

That sense of the divine breath in human deeds, creativity and suffering which had struck me so strongly as we looked at the North Sea through the interstices of Hambling's scallop, came once more. And it came more powerfully still as we looked at photographs of two young men in uniforms of the 1914-18 war which were on display in the church. These boys are buried in the churchyard, their lives cut down when they were just blossoming into adulthood, by the cruelty and folly of the powerful. Proud and a little self-conscious in their uniforms, they seem both far distant from us and yet familiar. They may not have had eloquent tongues in their lifetimes, but theirs are among the voices that will not be drowned.

Those voices, speaking across the centuries and continuing to speak in our own time, must be heard. It is our calling to listen. And I have learned during these few 'holy' days that it is necessary to occasionally stand back from the pursuit of what we may think to be contemporary, if our writing, speech and action is to retain relevance.

Places and Pondering

At a Performance of Messiah in Blythburgh Church

The spinning of wonder against the downdraught of the quotidian;
the casting of counterpoint into white-lit space,
these are clauses in a covenant
I strain to read.

Trumpets and tympani sounding beneath my feet
have lifted my eyes to
the Holy Host of Heaven, caught in wood and time
and forever horizontal to the affairs of men.

Below, mastery of mason and musician;
carvingcraft past and grace of skill present,
motion mind beyond dissolution.
I would learn.

The arts and anti-establishment scoundrels
March 3, 2017

As a direct result of the UK's decision to leave the EU, an internationally acclaimed orchestra is leaving Britain due to uncertainty as to the residency rights of its foreign players. The European Union Baroque Orchestra, which is based in Oxfordshire will relocate to Antwerp in May.

Emma Wilkinson, the orchestra's manager, fears other British-based orchestras may soon follow suit and that British musicians may find working in the remaining EU nations difficult while the Brexit negotiations take place.

The response of UKIP was predictable. A piece in UKIP Daily decided that this has "nothing to do with the people of Stoke and Copeland." Arron Banks tweeted "I'm sure that Labour voters in Stoke are devastated that a EU funded orchestra is leaving the UK."

This kind of reverse snobbery is not new. But it is perhaps being put to a new use in our increasingly divided society. The assumption that working class people are incapable of finding joy and inspiration in the arts is not just patronising and insulting, it is active exploitation of a deformed identity politics.

Like many of you who read this, I was born into the working class and educated into the middle class. That education was in no small part due to my family's love of music, literature and painting. We read poetry *cantoris et decani* around the fire on winter evenings, the music of brass bands and local choral societies sounded in my childhood aural memory and we would take long and often exhaustingly complicated journeys by bus and train to visit art galleries. The life-giving, even possibly life-saving, qualities of lining the heart and mind with as much as possible of the greatest which had been thought and written was impressed on me from an early age. "Learn poems by heart", my father once said to me; "if you were to be put in prison they would not let you have books." This was not an idle fancy. We were a family acquainted with the consequences of conscientious objection.

As politicians on both sides of the Atlantic increasingly see the dividing of communities and individuals as advantageous to power's pursuit and tenure, we must find means of building up what they would tear down. Communities will be well founded when they find sources of common joy. It is when we encounter something which takes us beyond ourselves and our circumstances, transfigures the commonplace and gives us what the Society of Friends call 'openings', that we are perhaps most authentically human. That moment of "what – you too? I thought I was the only one..." is a powerful tool for equality and justice as well as for personal enlargement.

My own leanings are perhaps more towards music and litera-ture than to the visual arts (but I have maps) and I trace my journey through the King James Bible, Shakespeare, Milton, Dickens and Bach. There have been singular moments of revelation in Arnold Bennett and Gustavo Flaubert and a continuing tumble of challenge in Schoenberg, Gerard Manley Hopkins and Geoffrey Hill. Only once did I hear the bum note of this not being for my station in life. But it did not echo for long because I learned that great art both transcends the conceits of small minds and celebrates a humanity which is recognisable wherever truth keeps the eyes wide. This is our common wealth.

Never let scoundrels in anti-establishment guise deceive you. Give us bread but give us roses.

A disturbing season
April 15, 2017

These are strange days for those of us whose spiritual lives are not focused on season and liturgy. The dramatic intensity of the Passion narrative is not to be denied, for non-credal Quakers, just as for athe-ists and devout church people.

Uncertain as I am about a bodily resurrection, I have no doubt about the incapacity of death and cruelty to end the power of Jesus' spirit. This is resurrection life – to live without being crushed or made de-spairing by the playing out of those forces which killed him and which endure in our own time.

The will and ability of power to encompass the destruction of those who are neither compliant nor apathetic has not changed greatly. It is 2000 years since the occupying power of a middle eastern coun-try, abetted by the religious establishment, decided that the radical preacher from a despised province was too disturbing to be tolerated. And today, perhaps more than ever, we know that truth is both fugitive and disturbing. It asks questions, requires ongoing re-framing of an-swers, inverts expectations and challenges us to look so much further than we are inclined to think possible.

Disturbance can bring great pain. Loss, betrayal, failure, self-loath-ing, guilt – these, and so many other backwashes of living in painful times, may break us. This is why for me, the only liturgy for this dis-turbing season is Bach's St Matthew Passion. At once monumental and tenderly intimate, it brings the universal into the here and the now.

And of all the wondrous music in this musical and spiritual masterpiece, it is the aria *Erbarme dich, mein Gott,* the grief of Peter when he realises he has denied Jesus, which most speaks to my mind and heart. The sorrowful discourse between the alto voice and solo violin is a place where the Divine plays in the theatre of our own experience.

The 'Mother of All Bombs', the lurching towards war, the persecution of difference and growing callousness towards the poor, the sick and the disabled are all spoken to here: "Have mercy on me, Lord my God, because of my weeping".

Whatever your spirituality, please spare a few minutes to take the possibility of encountering blessing in this wonderful combination of voice and instrument.

Gift

On my eighth birthday,
a rainbow stood over the steelworks.
Sevenlight, mounting and fading into gun-coloured sky
took the eye into immensity.
Imagination desired the arch complete and in that moment,
all the terraced town was small as a toy
and all the world a possibility.

The noise made by poetry and why power is afraid of it
April 9, 2015

Ask most parents what they want for their children and the answers will be overwhelmingly on the lines of wanting them to be happy, good, well-balanced and fulfilled individuals. The younger the child, the more likely this is to be centre frame.

As children advance through their education, concerns about enabling them to reach their full potential come more into play and at some stage, there will be a greater emphasis on what that might mean in terms of making a living.

What you are much less likely to hear, is an emphasis on defining any of these wishes in terms of a testing regime which seems to be sucking the life out of the joy of learning and driving teachers to exhaustion and despair.

The poet and children's novelist Michael Rosen recently wrote an open letter to the Education Secretary Nicky Morgan, demolishing the idea that children's reactions to a poem could be measured or confined to pre-determined interpretations.

The prescriptive and stultifying regime criticised by Rosen was not one intended for young people in their later teens, who might just have read and enjoyed enough poetry to be able to survive the purely technical interrogation of a text: it was a Key Stage 1 requirement – designed for seven and eight year olds.

This is an age where the imagination is lissom and tender – "wax to receive and marble to retain". If nurtured through sensitive teaching, it will blossom in a manner which lays a foundation for all disciplines.

Poetry, perhaps more than any other form of expression, shows, rather than tells a child that language can be playful, strange, mysterious and liberating. It sets ajar the door of original, independent thinking and does not always have to 'make sense'. A friend who is a teacher told me of once finding a boy generally thought 'unpromising', browsing a volume of Gerard Manley Hopkins. She asked him what he thought of these dense and brilliantly strange poems. "It's great, Miss", was his reply."I dunno what it means but I like the noise it makes." It is horrible to imagine what might have been done to that lad if Rosen's 'Mr Examiner' had grasped the breath of his nascent perception of beauty and throttled the life out of it in order to boost the youth to a Grade C GCSE pass and his school to a more advantageous position within a league table.

It is well known that Shelley believed poets to be "the unacknowledged legislators of the world". The preamble to this statement is not always heard: "[poets] are not only the authors of language and of music, of the dance, and architecture, and statuary, and painting; they are the instituters of laws, and the founders of civil society..." It is a bold claim, the meaning of which educationalists and politicians would do well to reflect upon. The tension between utilitarian education and liberal education is of long standing. Writing over 160 years ago, Dickens satirised the utilitarians who "see figures and averages and nothing else", in the horrible and ultimately piteous figure of the School Board Superintendent, Thomas Gradgrind.

This strangely timeless educational theorist could see nothing but inadequacy in little Sissy Jupe, a child of the circus, who did not know the definition of a horse ("Quadruped. Graminivorous. Forty teeth, namely twenty-four grinders, four eye-teeth, and twelve incisive. Sheds coat in the spring; in marshy countries, sheds hoofs, too. Hoofs hard, but requiring to be shod with iron. Age known by marks in mouth"). That she would carpet a floor with pictures of flowers and was later to be a kind friend to Gradgrind's own daughter was neither here nor there in his rigid and formulaic world-view.

If we are content that the needs of the CBI should be the driver of our education system and that as a consequence, only the narrowly measurable can be of value, we should not think ourselves more enlightened than this pinched parody figure who believed that only 'right' and 'wrong' answers could be possible in the realm of beauty and the imagination.

Poetry offers liberation. Neither children nor adults will always understand its meaning. But the capacity to relish the noise it makes renders it harder for power to oppress us. Perhaps that is why they would crush our children's earliest experiences of heightened and transformative language.

Roadworks

The road does not work ahead.
Curves of cones and narrowed lanes dislocate direction and intent:
road signs are made riddles and
I am disturbed by the immediacy of transience.

Custom becomes expectation.
Rumours of alteration go disregarded, unwelcome outliers,
messengers of change.
I shall be late.

And here, beneath rush-hour's easy irritation,
in conversancy overthrown, and recall teased,
clear and small
I catch the trickle of Lethe, tributary of Styx.

Fast lane to nowhere
October 2, 2011

"Slow down, you move too fast" In the 45 years which have passed since Paul Simon wrote the 59th Street Bridge Song, we have come to move a whole lot faster.

Web pages are expected to open in a nano-second, rail and air travel are judged, not by the reliability, safety or quality of the transit experience, but by the length of time taken to deliver a passenger from one hyper-ventilating city to another. And now, the government proposes to raise the motorway speed limit to 80 mph.

Acknowledging that this will mean more pollution, (fuel consumption and CO2 emissions up by 20 per cent), injuries and deaths, the government, in the person of the Transport Secretary Philip Hammond, nonetheless justifies the decision by the stunningly fatuous comment that the UK " needs to be back in the fast lane of global economics."

Governments can only perpetuate this kind of destructive idiocy because somewhere, deep down in our psyches, we have been willing to believe that fast equals success and that prosperity and status, both personal and national, may therefore be increased by arriving at destinations in a shorter time. Add this to the largely male concept of speed as an index of power and potency, and it is not difficult to see why Hammond's non sequitur may find an audience beyond the Clarkson tendency of neo-liberal marketeers.

But if we will step aside for a moment from the propaganda of those whom Greenpeace's head of media, Ben Stewart, has described as "nincompoops on crack", a smaller, quieter voice may just be heard reminding us that GDP is not the only measure of well-being, and that the implication that we must move over the surface of the planet at ever greater speeds unless we are to look like no-hopers, is more likely to lead to breakdown than to breakthrough.

The Quaker dictum "the simple life, freely chosen, is a source of strength" might have a chance of influencing the unquestioned acceleration of our consumerist rat-race if that freedom of choice could be made more accessible through a greater re-distribution of wealth and influence. And those of us who are fortunate enough to have a sufficiency – if not abundance – of means, need to heed the words of *Advices and Queries*: "seek to know an inward stillness, even amid the activities of daily life" if we are to play a part in re-calibrating our society's speed-fulfilment nexus.

Many of the fast-laners who are trapped on the hamster wheel of speed as the price for acquisition, spend large sums of money on counselling, health farms and other forms of stress-busting. This is the logic of madness and we need to challenge the orthodoxy which fails to question it. Refusing to worship at the altar of speed is a good place to start.

No abiding city: a parliament building for the 21st century?
September 16, 2016

The Palace of Westminster is falling down. The great Gothic fantasy on the north bank of the Thames is showing the wrinkles of its 150 years and is in urgent need of repair. The whole building is sinking, the stonework crumbling, the cabling is dangerously outdated and there is a considerable amount of asbestos within the building's fabric.

An independent report puts the cost of repair and restoration at £3.5 billion and the time scale at six years if MPs and peers were to be moved out. If the work were to be done with them *in situ*, the figures rise to £5.7 billion and 32 years respectively.

Either way, this is a great deal of money and entails a massive amount of disruption. There will no doubt be much enquiry and analysis as to the least-worst option.

But may we not see this as an opportunity to create a parliament building fit for the 21st century? The housing of an elected legislature should not be done on the cheap, because it is a symbol of how we think about the importance of democracy and governance. It should be architecturally and aesthetically valuable, equipped to deliver efficient processes and designed so as enable constructive debate, minimise ritual adversarialism and above all, to enhance transparent action by MPs and accountability to those who send them there.

The present House of Commons loves its traditions. For those of us outside the daily Westminster bubble, what is sometimes presented as a kind of validation of its longevity (in reality, amounting to only 150 years) appears at best dotty and at worst outright stupid. New MPs may have to wait weeks for an office and computer terminal but they are allocated a peg on which to hang their swords. The inherent misogyny will not go unremarked by female members. The opposing benches of the debating chamber with their 'two swords-length' of separation across the Despatch Box encourages rowdy and pointlessly confrontational behaviour. Legislatures (like places of worship) which sit in the round lose nothing in the pursuit of truth and justice but may gain much in respect, parity of esteem and mature behaviour.

Then there is technology. In a modern legislature – such as the Scottish Parliament – members vote from their seats. Electronic voting not only removes the cumbersome business of filing through the lobbies to be counted, it makes it far more likely that MPs will have been in the chamber to hear a least a part of the debate around the matter on which they are voting. It also minimises the opportunity for arm-twisting by the whips, thus restoring a balance between conscience and possible intimidation.

It is not without significance that the iconic building designed by Charles Barry and Augustus Pugin is in the Gothic revival style. The revisiting of the ecclesiastical style of the 14th century, so fashionable in the mid-Victorian era, was perceived as conferring the gravitas and authority of antiquity. Much that we claim as 'tradition' follows the same thinking and dates from the same period. Only consider some of the sentimental aspects of Christmas, often the subject of indignant defence from the Daily Mail school of theology, which are largely the invention of Prince Albert and Charles Dickens.

The Victorian-Gothic edifice in SW1 is recognised all over the world. It adorns sauce bottles, tea-towels and a great variety of tourist artefacts. That it stands on the site of the 13th century parliament of England should neither be discounted nor given too much weight. Valuing the past is not to be confused with its idolatrous worship. Here we have no abiding city, yet we frame what is to come within the geography of the temporal. It is recognising this that we may find a way to step away from the false allegiances which impede progress.

Perhaps the restoration of the fabric of a building which is no longer suitable as the home of the legislature could be re-imagined and re-made as a museum of the country's democratic and constitutional history and future. The often misquoted words of John Bright – a 19th century Quaker MP – are surely worth consideration. It is England, not Westminster which is the "mother of parliaments". That womb is not yet barren.

Calf Cop and the still dews of quietness
July 29, 2012

This morning I took part in Meeting for Worship in the small 18th century Friends Meeting House at Calf Cop in North Yorkshire. Situated in that area known to Quakers as '1652 country' where the borders of Yorkshire, Lancashire and Cumbria come within a few miles of each other, the Meeting House stands in a quiet burial ground bordered by pine trees and looks across an open landscape to the massive flat-topped mountain of Ingleborough.

It would be difficult to imagine a more peaceful setting. Access is via a footpath lying off a narrow lane which in turn, parts from a quiet minor road a few hundred yards below. The silence, both outside and within the Meeting House was profound. No traffic noise reaches here and the only external sounds were tiny threads of birdsong.

We heard of a Friend's sister who had died that night and were asked "to hold her soul in the Light and her family in our hearts with love and compassion." As a visitor, I had no personal knowledge of the family concerned, but this was a moment of great emotional power.

Reflecting on the generations of Friends who had sat in this building – and for whom such complete silence would have not been such a rare experience as it is for us today – I wondered how often they would have heard similar words. The mystery of the end of physical existence and the crushing experience of loss is the same in all generations. But I never before realised with quite such force how essential silence is to placing ourselves in a right relationship with suffering and incomprehension.

There is so much in our daily experience which is incomprehensible in its capacity to cause pain. We are buffeted by cruelty, greed, injustice, indifference to others and, it has to be said, by our own impotent anger. We may become aggressive, cynical or apathetic in response; we will almost certainly become stressed by the pace and pressure of modern life and by the troubles which come "not in single spies but in battalions."

We are about to enter on the month widely seen as being one of holiday, relaxation and re-creation. For myself, working with the reporting and analysis of news and comment upon current affairs, I have to consider what this means. I don't advocate idleness – I have health, strength and capacity and I need to make a living. But I am learning that occasionally standing back is essential, not just for perspective, but for emotional and spiritual health.

John Greenleaf Whittier's words from 'Dear Lord and Father of Mankind' – sometimes known as the 'Quaker hymn' came into my mind in that remote and beautiful little Meeting House this morning:

Drop thy still dews of quietness,
Till all our strivings cease;
Take from our souls the strain and stress,
And let our ordered lives confess
The beauty of thy peace.

It is a counsel of perfection and I shall fail more often than I succeed in receiving those gifts of quietness. But I shall remember Calf Cop and its gentle reminder that from time to time it is necessary to "attend to what love requires of you, which may not be great busyness."

Shipping Forecast

A cussed day. The burned toast,
the disappointing phone calls.
Landlocked, rigid, wet without fluidity.

The pavement gave no footspring;
the train transferred my position
without moving me.

But poem seeds drift on the edge
of sleep – Gibraltar to North Foreland,
squally showers, moderate to good, rising...

The sway of the sea is under me
and my bed trims to the wind.

Liminality: New Year, art and the rumour of Divinity
January 2, 2018

The strange betwixt-and-between period which separates Christmas from New Year is over. We have stepped through the exit of the old year and stand, uncertain, perhaps with hope, maybe in some anxiety, often in real fear, at the intake of 2018.

Liminality – derived from the Latin word for threshold, 'limin' – is not a condition to which we usually pay much attention. It is used to describe that quality of uncertainty, coupled with ambiguity, which is experienced mid-way through a ritual when the participant's former status has been laid down, but their post-ritual state has not yet been achieved.

It was at an undistinguished lay-by on the A1 during a recent journey from Cumbria to East Anglia, that I mused on social media about the slightly uneasy, but liberating sense of experiencing departure without yet having the consummation of arrival. A Twitter F/friend responded by drawing my attention to a 16th century painting which has now taken root in the life of my imagination.

Titian's immense oil, The Presentation of the Virgin at the Temple, depicts the mother of Jesus as a tiny child, hardly more than a toddler, ascending the steps of the Temple to where an elaborately dressed priest awaits her. The little girl holds up one side of her frock to keep from tripping and raises her other hand in that distinctively upright 'hello' gesture of very young children. She is at once fragile and self-possessed, taking the eye in a more immediate and lasting way than does the disproportionally towering figure of the priest at the head of the steps. His arms are raised in a movement which combines ceremony with an element of astonishment. It is oddly tender.

The child, as yet without knowledge of what is to come, nor of quite what is happening in the moment, is evidently doing that which is required of her. Here is a sense of the unavoidable taking hands with transformative potential which I find deeply moving and which opens a door into that region where the Divine comes close: "Over again, I feel thy finger and find thee".

That the account of Mary coming to the Temple is held to be unhistorical, appearing not in canonical scripture but in the Protoevangelium of James, adds to its power as part of mythic truth. This is the universal language of the heart and not of the textual choices of authority. The skill and vision of a great artist has made this available to us and it is the creative response of creature to Creator which, opening the heart and the mind, may yet startle us with the rumour of Divinity.

Poetry, music, visual art, these have the power to open us and to create 'thin places' between our state of being and that which is 'beyond' – name it as you will. There is another significant figure in Titian's painting: an old woman seated at the side of the Temple steps is selling eggs. She looks in the opposite direction to the event occurring above and behind her – her attitude less one of uninterest than of complete unawareness.

Most of us need to 'sell eggs'. But if it is to the exclusion of wonder, of the potential to encounter the transformative, then we are poor indeed. Whatever happens in 2018, let us try always to make room for the beautiful, the challenging and the unexpected.

Kennings

The skald sang. Of longships
winnowing wave-meadows,
of waiting love shore-left,
 the breast-hoard fallen far
behind the wild whale's-acre.

Across twelve hundred years
I hear his tongue, test his
words on farm gates, way-posts,
treading his earth, heart-kent.

Patriotism and *heimat*: the geography of our common humanity
May 17, 2017

Samuel Johnson's epithet does not mean that all patriots are scoundrels. It invites us rather to consider the uses to which scoundrelly intent may put the concept.

But first, what might patriotism be? Is it useful? I love my country but I would hesitate to call myself a patriot. This is largely because I fear that to be an idea which has been hijacked and prised away from its gentler virtues. I am an English-born woman of mixed descent. Polish Jews, Ulster Scots and Bavarians have all laid their markers in my genes. But England is where I hatched. And – as with a duckling – it is the early imprint which influences attachment.

This attachment is measured in landscape, in legend, history, music and literature. It nourishes me in small northern towns with their ageless music of dialect and in the rapidly shifting polyglot hum of large cities. It is perhaps most dear in the whine of winds through the coarse grass sieves of high fells, the cry of a curlew or the glimpse of a tiny silver tarn beneath crags and screes. It has nothing to do with a flag, a head of state or with military pageantry.

It is rooted a sense of place and that is why the German word *heimat* means more to me than mother/father/home/land. There is no precise translation of this word and it carries no baggage of power or exclusion. It expresses that lift of the heart which is experienced when we return to a beloved place after long absence and when memories formed in that place come tumbling back.

Places are as much of the mind and heart as of maps and languages. Elgar and Bach have a common *heimat* as do Arnold Bennett and Arundhati Roy. This is the location where we may be taken not just 'out of' but beyond ourselves. And it is in that territory that we find more about our common being and move away from the smallness of defining ourselves by what we are not. It is a land which is not hospitable to exceptionalism, racism, xenophobia or any other divisive hauteur.

It is a great pity, though not altogether surprising, that Theresa May chose to weaponise an impoverished concept of patriotism to attack Jeremy Corbyn last week. She accused him of "abandoning the patriotic working class". As she can know little of the Labour leader's inner relationship with his native place, she would appear to have based her judgement on his once being seen to refrain from singing the National Anthem, on his belief that armed force should be a last resort, undertaken in accordance with international law when all else has failed, and on his refusal to facilitate nuclear annihilation. Such shallow, partial metrics are the tools of a particular type of narrow and intolerant nationalism. And they are no more characteristic of the working class than of any other stratum of society.

If more politicians would have the courage to step away from this kind of opportunistic reductionism and to explore the common riches of *heimat*, we could take a significant step towards a more just and inclusive society. The idolatry of outward forms has nothing to say to the commonwealth of our humanity. That is a different geography.

A sense of place and nationalism resisted
May 21, 2014

On the eve of the European elections, patriotism – or at least politicians' appropriation of that condition – is much in the air. I shall refrain from any temptation to refer to scoundrelly tendencies and consider instead, the gentler, and what I believe to be the more fruitful concept of a 'sense of place.'

There will be few of us who have not experienced the awareness of the indivisibility of a landscape or urban space with something deep-rooted and nourishing. It may be aesthetic – the music of Benjamin Britten and the long, shingled littoral of Suffolk; it may be John Clare's lyrical and melancholic evocations of the woods and pathways around his Helpston home, or the mill-scapes and spindly figures of Lowry's industrial north country. Perhaps it will manifest in a sense of wonder at the ingenuity of the technical genius and vision of those who spanned the river at Ironbridge Gorge and built Ribblehead viaduct. These are some of my reference points as an Englishwoman. They remind me that I cannot be alone in knowing myself as not only rooted in, but taking meaning and awareness of possibility from familiar surroundings.

It is these different experiences which form our emotional and spiritual responses and invite us to reflection on how we may use them in solidarity, in justice, in incarnating what it means to be human in the cultures and locations in which we are placed.

And lest that should sound like an audition for Pseud's Corner, let's remember that those who would make fellow citizens and sharers of our space into the 'other' or seek to persuade us that they can't share what is universal because they look different, call their Creator by another name, have a memory of other landscapes, or even live north of Carlisle, impoverish what we already have in common and diminish what we might become.

Power may like to claim its postcode, but people know better when they listen to the truth of experience and acknowledge its universality with generosity. The mean-spirited introversion of nationalism and patriotism perverted which would blind us to this must be resisted.

Among Friends

In a Meeting House Garden

On a slender bench beneath George Fox's apple tree,
this summer's afternoon, I am.

Behind me, Friends long passed through the place a final time,
lie beneath low stones.

And all along the path, fat bees among the grey and green
of lavender, populate the still air with purposed hum.

Flesh, bones, fruit and spirit. Quietness and enterprise.
So it ever was and long will be.

I am glad I was here.

George Fox, Jeremy Corbyn and the value of waiting
October 4, 2015

> 'Up wi' thee, George', says God. And being up,
> He saw the Lancashire sea, and God's people,
> Waiting to be found.

Thus UA Fanthorpe describes the start of George Fox' s mission in her poem 'Fox Unearthed'.

Having just taken a few days holiday (for the first time in perhaps too long), I find these words much in my mind. Being up, and waiting are opposing states and most of us are better at the former.

Our work culture affords status to the density of our engagement diaries, to influence measured in appearances of opinion, to miles covered and length of hours worked. We all know people who are ever 'up' and in motion and assume that this must equate with utility or achievement. We may be one of those people. We may also be mistaken.

Waiting, on the other hand, implies passivity, a lack of initiative or ambition. The balance is not easy to find and although Quakers have been both described as contemplative activists and active contemplatives, we are the products of a common culture and may find that balance as difficult as anyone else.

But last week, walking by the Cumbrian sea and in "the high, the muddy, the beastly places" where George Fox "shins up further Firbank/ Drinks water, preaches to a thousand", having deleted all work-related emails from my phone unread and unplugged myself as far as possible from the news-cycle, I began to find space to reflect on the challenges and virtues of waiting. Not just waiting to be 'found' personally, but also of waiting in the sense of understanding the importance of allowing matters to unfold into the finding of possibility and promise before engaging in too much analysis, comment or opinion fixing.

That may sound like a uniquely commentariat-centred problem. But it really isn't. We take decisions, pass comment and formulate opinions every day of our lives, whatever our trade. And some of those decisions may have to be taken quickly if we are to be effective, or even safe in our dealings. We have livings to get and 'up' is most certainly not an inferior state. But it may all too easily become a self-defeating and destructive one if it never factors in the 'waiting' with its attendant humility and awareness that the instant opinion may so easily harden into the long term prejudice.

Some of the barrel-scraping comment which has shamed ink and airwaves in the three weeks since Jeremy Corbyn was elected leader of the Labour Party has illustrated this danger in a manner which would be comical if it were not so damaging to our understanding of a newly evolving democratic climate. One piece of absurd confirmation bias stimulates the next, which in its turn forms the foundation for building prophecies of doom and destruction. It does not take long for this structure to become the norm from which everyone starts to take their bearings, for or against. That it may be a house built on sand may escape us in our anxiety to find a comfort zone cemented by the group think of our tribe (and non-conformists are just as vulnerable to this intellectual seduction as Establishment thinkers). Standing back a little may not save us entirely from such failure, but the exercise of waiting may just be more profitable than the less thoughtful drivings of unexamined 'up'.

I am grateful to a Tweet-mate who helped me sift my thoughts on Fanthorpe's poem by pointing out uniquely how she grasps George Fox's character. *Fox Unearthed* – possibly better than any biographical study – catches the quality of journeying and change in the life of a man who managed a pretty good balance between the being up and the waiting. She understands the significance of his evolution from a lonely, confused teenager to a much loved, spiritually and morally mature man who, shortly before his death, was able to say "I am glad I was here". Significantly, he added: "Now I am clear. I am fully clear" – in a context which shames politicians' frequent and clichéd use of that term.

If we would be fully clear, if we would seek truth rather than follow the promptings of ego, we need to avoid equally the pitfalls of quietism and the idolatry of relentless activity.

On Reburying Bones at Settle Meeting House

(Remains of Friends were unearthed when foundations were laid for an extension to the Meeting House at Settle, North Yorkshire in 2004)

Touching silence, nudged by mortality,
we listened to the reading of names.
Calling Friends, naming them friends
across three hundred years:
Robert, Isaac, Jennet; noun to memory,
identity to presence. Only stillness sufficed.
Outside, motion returned. Hand to hand, the spade
became an instrument of sacrament; all were priested, all
stood equal in manifesting mystery.

Limestone land took them back; minerals of men to
their making earth and we, the passing ones,
graced with time enough for gentle duty,
dispersed in rinsing rain.

A Quaker communion of saints
October 4 2010

The Communion of Saints is not a term which comes readily to a Quaker's tongue. But an encounter with two Friends – one living and one three centuries dead – has prompted me to look past the difficulty of these words in search of their true meaning.

We had passed a long weekend walking the Cumbrian fells and our last day was spent in the Howgills – those striking uplands which make the stretch of the M6 between Kendal and Shap so memorable and unique.

The Cross Keys pub, a temperance inn, stands at the foot of Cautley Spout on the road between Sedbergh and Kirkby Stephen. This is the heart of '1652 country' – those parts of Cumbria, Westmorland and North Yorkshire where Quakerism has such deep roots. Nearby are Brigg Flatts Meeting House and Firbank Fell where George Fox preached to a gathering of thousands and "convinced many". I should not therefore, have been surprised to discover that the Cross Keys was kept by a 'vociferous Quaker', Alan Clowes. Alan greeted me after the manner of Friends and we were soon in easy and delightful conversation. But I was a bit startled when he told me that "Dorothy Benson stays with us".

Dorothy was one of the 'valiant sixty', a group of ordinary men and women, farmers, tradesmen and shopkeepers, also known as the 'first publishers of the truth' – itinerant preachers who spread the ideas of Friends throughout England, Europe and the New World in the latter half of the 17th century. These early exponents of radical religion and civil disobedience frequently ran foul of the authorities and suffered for it. Dorothy was no exception. She was imprisoned for arguing with a cleric of the Established Church during a service and gave birth to her son Immanuel while in jail. She died soon after her release and as was the custom amongst Friends at that time, was buried, not in consecrated ground, but in garden of the family home – the house which was to become the Cross Keys Inn.

When the inn was extended in the 18th century, part of the garden was built over and Dorothy's grave lies under the modern dining area. Alan told me that visitors often ask, in the idiom of the area, if Dorothy "comes around". "Nay, she doesn't" he said. "She's at peace." (And among Friends.)

The wholly unlooked for experience of such a warm meeting with another Quaker and of knowing that an extraordinarily brave exponent of our faith was resting beneath us, was a deeply moving reminder of the Quakerly admonition "seek to know one another in the things which are eternal." And as we talked the afternoon away, I had a growing sense of a continuum of belief and practice which runs from Dorothy Benson's time to our own.

The project which Alan Clowes and his wife Chris run in South Africa, creating jobs, skills and sustainable opportunities in an area of great deprivation, is part of a connectivity and love which cannot be changed by death or by time and which is upheld by the witness of those who have preceded us. If that is the Communion of Saints, then sign me up.

Our Friend Writes a Minute

(The Quaker Clerk)

Task's tools laid workmanlike:
pad squared to the table and
pen edge-straight – a grid
for capture.

We are silent.
It takes time, this spirit catching, this
wording of our mind.
– Friends, I have a minute.
We hope so.

On endings, beginnings and calling things by their right names
January 12, 2017

T.S. Eliot is the poet of endings and beginnings and of the paradoxes which dwell within that cycle. These words from Little Gidding seem particularly worthy of consideration as we enter a time of considerable and – let it be said – disturbing change:

> For last year's words belong to last year's language
> And next year's words await another voice.

What that voice may be is a question for every one of us. Will we respond to bigotry and xenophobia with an aggression which undermines what it should promote and devalues the quality of opposition? How will we react to the frequently intemperate and ill-informed world of social media? How ready are we to accept the moral shortcuts which are increasingly becoming the currency of 140-character rants?

Behind such questions looms the pernicious delusion that we now live in a 'post-truth' age. 'Another voice' must learn to call manifestations of this shameless piece of laziness what they are – lies. And of course, power has always lied. There is nothing new about that. But by acquiescing in this definition with its slightly pretentious tone (remember 'the end of history'?) we make ourselves passive recipients of both deceit and an abandoning of the redemptive, transformative quality of being ashamed.

In the same manner, 'fake news' must be named, without fear, as propaganda. Apart from its increasing tendency to mean whatever Donald Trump finds inconvenient, it will be a deep shame on all free societies if we permit the concept to generate cynicism in place of sceptical enquiry and discernment. If we poison the wells of even the possibility of journalistic integrity, we will have neither defence against tyranny nor aspiration to freedom with justice. Those of us who work in the media must redouble our efforts to be publishers of truth, to research, to verify, to check and check again and above all, to resist the lemming-rush to responses which value speed above discernment.

Last year's words may belong to last year's language, but do the emotional worlds of Shakespeare and Milton no longer communicate with that which has depth and worth in our spirits? Let us never confuse register with truth because, as a Chinese proverb reminds us,

"The beginning of wisdom is to call things by their right names". This is surely how we may

> ...arrive where we started
> And know the place for the first time.

Turning towards 'stayedness': George Fox's rebuke to our current politics
July 21, 2016

I am not a member of the Labour Party. But when Jeremy Corbyn was elected leader with a huge mandate in September 2015, I felt a renewal of hope.

Hope that politics might escape its Westminster-centric bubble; hope for a more truthful and less pointlessly confrontational politics; hope that the party might be moved away from its focus-group oriented form of cautious neo-liberalism. And above all, hope that those who most need hope in our divided and unequal society might have it restored to them.

But it has not worked out that way. There is fault on both sides. Jeremy Corbyn's many and considerable virtues are deeply attractive to many of us – he seems to me to have the Quaker Testimonies of peace, equality, simplicity and truth at his heart – but nothing in his political career has prepared him for leadership. He is more at home with campaigning and protest than with managing a parliamentary group with the compromises and collegiality which that entails. His failure in this regard has left the government unopposed for too long.

The parliamentary party is arguably at greater fault. From – literally – the moment of Corbyn's acceptance speech, too many of its members have sniped, leaked, misrepresented and sought to undermine their leader. There appears to have been little effort to seek dialogue or to find means of co-operation and amendment for a greater good. The mismanaged 'chicken-coup' was the sorry outcome of this.

Vitriol, lies and half-truths have taken hold in the party to an extent where it has become all but impossible to see many MPs and Labour members working together again with any kind of trust. And at a time of 'post-fact' and 'post-truth' politics, the electorate is still further disillusioned and more than ready to seek out and publicise any inconsistency in the statements, voting records and policy positions of prominent politicians.

Although it is important to acknowledge that most of us will make changes in our stances and interpretations as our thinking evolves over the years, there is a footloose 'flexibility' in many politicians which enables them to swing through 180 degrees in a startlingly short space of time if they perceive it as useful to their cause.

One of Jeremy Corbyn's greatest strengths is his consistency. He is without the streak of opportunism common in his trade because he has firm principles to which he has adhered throughout three decades of elected service. This characteristic is a significant part of his appeal to many people and it is a quality often lacking in public life. Our culture tends towards admiration of the fast moving and is given to confusing change with progress. Popularity – in many ways inimical to integrity – is more highly prized than steadfastness and constancy. Indeed, these words have an old-fashioned ring to them. And to be thought outdated or uncool is not on the wish-list of most politicians.

The present political climate is volatile, ugly and destabilising. Cynicism and despair are greatly in evidence and affect us all to some degree. The need to stand back, to disengage from the anger in order to find a more constructive and sober perspective presses upon the spirit. George Fox's admonition, "Be still and cool in thy own mind and spirit from thy own thoughts" is as valuable now as it was three hundred years ago. And it is in words which arrest the attention precisely because they are 'old-fashioned' and not the language of advertising or political group-think, that he continues by turning our minds towards that strength which may "allay all tempests, against blusterings and storms. That is it which moulds up into patience, into innocency, into soberness, into stillness, into stayedness, into quietness, up to God, with his power."

You do not have to be a theist to feel the timeless and needful qualities of soberness, stillness and above all, of "stayedness" All of us, politicians and electorate, would do well to stay our minds on truth and on principle.

In praise of standing back
May 12, 2018

Responses to the results of last week's local elections offer a cautionary tale about the impulse to rush into comment and justification. The number and extraordinary ingenuity of the ongoing claims, counter-claims and sheer magical thinking has been absurd – by turns comical and dispiriting.

However, this level of elaborately spun flight from the uncertainties of complex and still evolving circumstances is by no means the private territory of politicians. There are a great many reasons why almost all of us will, at some time, fall into a similar temptation.

Our culture does not take kindly to delay in expressing an opinion or to admitting that we may not yet have one. Caution is not exciting; watching and reflection do not play into an impoverished but popular concept of conviction; the urge to hang views in the Twittersphere, on air or in print is a badge of being informed, of being – according to the mores of our own group – far too smart to be taken in by 'the other side'.

Martin Luther's "Hier stehe ich. Ich kann nicht anders" – the iconic statement of principled non-conformity which still has the power to raise goosebumps across 500 years – was not an angry or reflexive riposte in a binary conflict. It was a voice of calm, raised in reasoned defence of the books he had written which pleased neither Pope or Emperor: books which were the outcome of years of evolving thought and struggles with conscience. Whether he was right or wrong, is in so many ways, secondary to the measure of the thing.

The clock-spring of our own time is wound differently. Its coil bends to gratification in the moment. The comforts of 'winning'; of demolishing another's argument; of shoring up one's own standing – maybe even of whistling in the dark, because confirmation bias flourishes where there is fear – cannot be denied.

Some confrontation is an inevitable part of dissent. But if it is not well founded in fact and truth, it quickly becomes damaging and futile in its hostility. One unevidenced claim sparks another and the spiral into insult may occur with frightening speed and consequent further obfuscation. As protagonists dig into their entrenchments, this becomes the territory where 'fake news' and 'alternative facts' demolish trust and render the conversation meaningless.

To stand back and to admit that one does not yet know is not to opt out of taking a moral stance. It may in itself be a manifestation of morality in pursuit of truth. To declare certainty without regard to nuance, misinformation or sheer confusion, is not a virtuous action. The fence may be a wise place upon which to sit a while when travelling towards the standfast.

The Waypost of James Nayler

There is a spirit that delights to do no evil,
persistent and tender, it rises through cracks in concrete
to hollyhock bloom.
It will bubble, lithe and unforeseen
as mercury in muddy earth,
such is the ground and spring of truth's self-nature
neither owning nor owing other.

Hoping to outlive wrath and contention,
it hunkers, plain clad and lacking looks, in unregarded places,
waiting for hauteur to outwear
and dwindle, spindling to futility and dust.
It gazes on temptation's horizon
then, being light-burdened,
spreads its map once more.

It takes its kingdom with entreaty and not with contention,
husbanding its land with lowliness of mind,
its grain sown in sorrow's sweat
but springing to lives' bread.
Walk with me, Friend.

Schadenfreude and the spirit
January 18, 2012

Schadenfreude is a disagreeable trait in human nature. But most of us will at some time have fallen victim to the spiteful little voice which ricochets around the outer edges of our consciences, whispering gleefully, "Good. Serves them right."

Religious schadenfreude is even more to be deplored because it is so contrary to the transformative love which should always be our lodestar. To wish for or to take pleasure in others' pain or discomfiture, however opposed to their ideas and behaviour I might be, is to increase the amount of hostility in the world and to do nothing for reconciliation or an increase of understanding.

The small campaign group Christian Voice has claimed that Tesco's poor Christmas trading figures and the consequent drop in its share value was the result of "divine intervention". This attribution of malign intent to the divine is apparently the result of Christian Voice's prayer for "confusion in the Tesco boardroom". Fortunately, this tells us more about the attitude of those who believe God endorses their views, however narrow those may be, than about the love that moves the stars and which found personification in a radical Palestinian preacher.

There are many reasons to be uneasy about the power exercised by Tesco. For many of us, their financial support for a family area at Gay Pride is not one of them. Christian Voice take a different view and provided they do not encourage prejudice or foment hatred, they are at liberty to do so. But to pray deliberately for difficulties and to exult in a situation which may lead to redundancies and hardship for employees who are not highly paid, is not just vindictive, it is to abdicate responsibility for working as agents of respectful communication and possible change.

Tesco's increasing monopoly in so many retail areas, its capacity to impose harsh conditions on small suppliers, the deleterious effect on local communities of its land bank holdings and out of town expansion are in many ways a microcosm of an economic system increasingly perceived as profoundly unjust. This is where Christian voices should – and are – being raised. But to focus on a particular view of sexuality to the apparent exclusion of social and economic justice, and to pray for destruction instead of campaigning for change from a standpoint which seeks healing and solutions, is surely to have parted from the spirit.

That spirit has no part with vengefulness and takes no delight in punishment or misfortune. It was wonderfully displayed in the witness of James Nayler as he lay dying in 1660 after being beaten and robbed: "There is a spirit which I feel that delights to do no evil, nor to revenge any wrong, but delights to endure all things, in hope to enjoy its own in the end. Its hope is to outlive all wrath and contention, and to weary out all exaltation and cruelty, or whatever is of a nature contrary to itself. It sees to the end of all temptations. As it bears no evil in itself, so it conceives none in thought to any other... it takes its kingdom with entreaty and not with contention, and keeps it by lowliness of mind."

Those words are treasured by Quakers and, I believe, are at the heart of so much that is good in the thinking and action of all people of good faith. We all need to guard ourselves from any temptation to mistake conviction for infallibility, retribution for justice or undiscerning satisfaction for righteousness.

Cultivating the discipline of peace
October 8, 2009

Quakerism is a non-credal faith having neither magisterium or hierarchy. That its ethos survives, coheres and continues to develop, is in no small part due to the central Testimonies against which Quakers, both corporately and as individuals, constantly check and challenge their lives.

The four core Testimonies are peace, equality, simplicity and truth. In recent years, some Friends have added community and the environment but I do not include these as I believe they can be understood as part of the requirement to live in equality and with simplicity.

By far the best known of the Testimonies is that of peace. Quakers are recognised as 'peace people' even amongst those whose knowledge of Friends is limited to a vague perception that we wear broad-brimmed black hats and subsist on porridge.

The witness of Friends to pacifism and peace-making reaches from their declaration to Charles II in 1660 – "all bloody principles and practises we do utterly deny...the spirit of Christ which leads us all into Truth will never move us to fight and war against any man with outward weapons" – to present day peace-maker teams and activists opposed to the conflict in Afghanistan.

Historically, many Friends have paid a heavy price in imprisonment, courts martial, disgrace and persecution even though conscientious objectors have, in times of conscription, served in the Friends' Ambulance Unit and other humanitarian organisations.

But just as the Testimonies are not fixed forms of words or static statements of dogma, the definition of peace should not be limited to an absence of war. Conflict, in many guises, presents itself in families, workplaces, friendships, occasions of recreation, local streets and worshipping communities.

Advices and Queries – a small book of discipline which has served the Society of Friends as a collective and personal guide to the examination of conscience and conduct for over three centuries – contains this searching admonition: "Bring into God's light those emotions, attitudes and prejudices in yourself which lie at the root of destructive conflict, acknowledging your need for forgiveness and grace."

Because there is a tendency in human nature to file difference under categories of black and white, right and wrong, we may easily fall into indignation, outrage or contempt when met with opposition in its various forms. There are many snares for our feet: "I have conviction, you have prejudices"; the temptation to assume oneself more intelligent or better informed than one's opponent; the tone-deafness which makes us insensitive to experience or culture at odds with our own and, most damagingly, the ugly and immature desire to have the last word and emerge as the 'winner'. And all this before any abusive or aggressive behaviour may have been displayed.

It is in permitting these apparently low-key conflicts to go unexamined and in preferring dominance over resolution, that the seeds of resentment and anger are sown. When these destructive emotions are fed by a sense of dis-empowerment, violence of emotion may eventually lead to physical violence.

Bringing my own attitudes into the light makes it more likely that I will learn to show respect for different views and discover the humility to give root-room for the dialogue which is essential if mutual trust is to grow.

Advices and Queries also reminds Quakers to "think it possible you may be mistaken" when dealing with the unfamiliar or with attitudes which may trouble us. Without insight into my own weaknesses, I am unlikely to play a part in creating a space where understanding and forbearance make possible the peaceful outcomes which enable us all to grow.

To have a heart and mind disposed towards peace, it is important to seek the condition of peace as understood in phrases such as "a bit of peace and quiet" or "just leave me in peace for a while". Our culture tends towards constant stimulus. It is loud, fast and frequently lacks nuance.

Occasional retreat from this destructive ambience is essential if we are to learn the habit of alert attentiveness to the ways of true peace. A few days walking fells or coastal paths may serve, but a simpler discipline can be woven into our working and family life – the occasional unplugging from electronic devices of communication or entertainment, a short withdrawal to garden or private space, a determination to spend a few minutes each day in silent solitude, these are all opportunities for the Divine to touch our inner being and gradually transform our thinking.

It has been well said that peace is not the absence of noise, trouble or hard work – rather it is to be in the midst of those things and still be calm in your heart.

Epilogue

After a Sleepless Night

Once, when a child played on a pipe,
reedsound, in wires of blue and silver
would flow down fell sides
to pool in dales below.
In that time, words could dance
pin sharp on the heads of angels
and the rhymes of lovers were
rich and rowan red
on the unmapped mountain sides.
Never such seamless ease again
since the Muses learned to write.

About Ekklesia

Ekklesia is an independent network providing 'thought space' for exploring the impact of ethics and beliefs in the areas of public and social policy.

We want to encourage transformative local engagement with global issues – not least among moral communities (churches and other groups) who see themselves as being firmly committed to people at the margins.

Our operational values are those of social justice, inclusion, nonviolence, environmental action, participative democracy and creative exchange among those of different convictions (religious or otherwise).

Ekklesia is active in promoting – alongside others – new models of mutual economy, conflict transformation, peacemaking, social power, restorative justice, citizen action and truth-telling in public life. This means moving beyond 'top-down', colonial approaches to politics, economics and beliefs.

While strongly influenced by the Peace Churches and grassroots movements for social change, Ekklesia is keen to work with people of many backgrounds who share common principles and approaches.

Ekklesia's reports, news analysis and commentary can be accessed via our website (www.ekklesia.co.uk) on Twitter (Ekklesia_co_uk) and on Facebook (www.facebook.com/ekklesiathinktank/).

About Siglum

Siglum is a new imprint from Ekklesia Publishing that focuses on the illuminative and transformative possibilities of the arts, music and culture in both religious and secular contexts. Its logo is a dove, the universal sign of peace.

Lightning Source UK Ltd.
Milton Keynes UK
UKHW010943130821
388804UK00001B/23

9 780993 294280